About A Scarlet

"I love the vulnerability and courage of this book. As we journey with Sheryl Griffin through her very painful past, a past that all but destroyed her, we see glimmers of God's goodness and faithfulness as He reaches down and lifts her up out of the pit and into a new and bright place of love, healing, and redemption. A powerful story and a must-read for anyone who's ever felt battered and broken down by life."

Susy Flory, Author of *So Long Status Quo:*
What I Learned From Women Who Changed the World

"This book had me hooked from the first page. It is not only a compelling story about Sheryl's life and what God has brought her through but also, having recently experienced my own panic attack, this book helped me unravel a few of the mysteries in my own life . When I started reading it, I couldn't put it down and as I finished it, I felt richer for sharing in such a journey."

Cindy Morgan
Christian Singer, Songwriter, Author

"It has been remarkable to watch Sheryl bravely walk through the process of facing her painful past. Only God could have orchestrated the timing of all of this so that Sheryl could begin to truly breathe again, to use her story to help others and then to seal the deal – He made sure the enemy didn't have the final say over the circumstances of her past. AMEN!!"

Kim Bindel Ford, Salem Radio Network Morning Show Host

"Knowing Sheryl's struggles makes her survival and triumph that much sweeter. Congratulations to a very courageous woman."

Anne Fottrell, M.D.

"Women from all walks of life will be able to relate to *A Scarlet Cord of Hope*. Sheryl is a wonderful new author, and I can't wait for her next book!"

Annie Brown

"In this book Sheryl takes you on a journey and shows how God can take anything and use it for His purpose. As someone who has seen first hand her strength of character and the love of Christ she shows others through her everyday life I would highly recommend this book to everyone, no matter what you're going through, the testimony in this book proves God is in control."

Stephen Belk

"Sheryl was the leader of a women's Bible study, *Bad Girls of the Bible,* at our church several years ago. Through her openness and honesty, she led so many of us to a freeing release of guilt and feeling completely forgiven. She is one of the strongest and most sincere Christian women I know, and has a talent for nurturing others with her encouraging words."

Carole Douglas

"After 30-years of friendship, one thing I know about Sheryl is that she loves the Lord her God with all her heart, with all her mind and with all her soul. *A Scarlet Cord of Hope* is not only Sheryl's testimony but reveals how God can intricately weave healing, faith, and restoration, for all who believe."

Monica Cane, Author of *The Lost Coin*

"I am inspired by passionate people who allow their own vulnerability to encourage and inspire others. Sheryl personifies this in both her personal walk of faith, and in this book. It's a blessing to watch her persist in the midst of personal trials, and succeed. This book will provide much needed courage to many women whose wells of hope have run dry. "

Suzette Greer, Motivational Speaker, TheBalancedHome.com

A Scarlet Cord of Hope

My Journey through Guilt, Shame, and Fear to Hope

By Sheryl Griffin

PUBLISHED BY WESTVIEW, INC., NASHVILLE, TENNESSEE

PUBLISHED BY WESTVIEW, INC.
P.O. Box 210183
Nashville, Tennessee 37221
www.publishedbywestview.com

ISBN 978-1-935271-30-7

First edition, January 2010

Biblical quotations from the New American Standard Bible.

Back cover photo by Elise Inman Photography.

Printed in the United States of America on acid free paper.

www.SherylGriffin.com

Sheryl@SherylGriffin.com

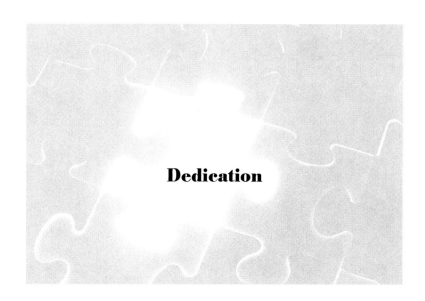

Dedication

This book is for my daughter Lauren and my son Garic. May you hold firmly to the grace and knowledge of Jesus Christ and know that a scarlet cord does not have to weigh you down- there is always HOPE. I'll love you forever; I'll like you for always. oxox

This book is also dedicated to my husband Doug. You are my Knight In Shining Armor. 143. oxox

Acknowledgments

I would like to first thank Jesus Christ for paying the ultimate price for my sin, my scarlet cord. Thank you Jesus, for loving me unconditionally. Thank you for giving me hope. I also want to thank my wonderful husband Doug who has always encouraged and supported me. I am grateful for our relationship. Thank you for being a man of integrity and for always telling me how I still check all of your boxes. Thank you for always believing in me and cheering me on, and of course, for making me laugh, especially during the tough times. I am also very grateful for my children Lauren and Garic. You give me hope and joy every day. Thank you for your patience as I grew through this process. Thank you for loving me, trusting me, and encouraging me. Lauren, thank you for helping me come up with the title and for your concept and idea on the sparrow. You helped make my book official!

I would also like to thank the following people who have mentored, encouraged, edited, or prayed for me as I went on this journey as I kept saying, "I am not a writer, I am only a woman with a story."

Monica Cane – We have journeyed through a lot together. Thank you for all of your encouragement, wisdom, prayers, and advice. Thank you for taking time to mentor me and share your own experiences with me as I began to write. My prayer is that someday we will be able to minister to other women, side by side together. Thank you for being my friend.

Lisa Wood – You are a true friend. You have always been an example of a Proverbs 31 woman to me. Thank you for writing that letter to me. Thank you for always praying for me. Thank you for taking time to read my manuscript and respond to me, even with everything that was swirling around you at that time. I love you like a sister!

Linda Bonk-Jackson – A dear friend whom I have known since the 9th grade. We are more alike than you ever knew. You have always been a loyal loving friend to me. I appreciate you! Your friendship means a lot to me. I treasure the time you took to read and edit my manuscript. Thank you!

Susy Flory – I am so grateful that God connected us. You are an amazing writer. You inspire me! Thank you for your belief in my story and me. Thank you for all of the emails you took time to read and respond too. I look forward to meeting you in person someday so I can hug you! Thank you!

Cindy Morgan – Who would have guessed after being Olivia's preschool teacher all those years ago that we would connect once again through my manuscript. God is good! Thank you so much for all of your input, encouragement, and prayers as I worked through the final edits. Your support was a blessing. I am grateful for your friendship! Thank you for challenging me to dig deeper and add more.

Michelle Griffin – My Mother in Law – thank you for taking time to read my manuscript. I appreciate your input, support, and encouragement. I love you MiL!

Shelli Tinsley – My sister – "gril," we have been through a lot together. I love you! Thank you for reading my manuscript. I know it was hard. Thank you for gently pointing out the corrections needed for accuracy. Thank you for your openness and courage as we opened the door that had not been opened in a long time. Thank you for always loving me and trusting me. I am grateful for our relationship.

Melanie – aka Auntie Mel and EB2 – My sister – I am very grateful for our relationship. I appreciate your encouragement and support in my writing (and in my life). Thank you for inspiring me to consider what the actual puzzle would look like in the end. You are one of the most talented and gifted women that I know – I am not just saying that because you make me incredibly beautiful jewelry – I mean it! EB1 over and out

Sylvia Simpson and Stacey Lamont – my favorite aunt and my favorite cousin – thank you both for reading my manuscript and for encouraging me. I love you both. I wish we lived closer. I am still looking forward to a girl's trip with you both.

Mary Catharine Nelson – Thank you for sharing your story with me, inspiring me, encouraging me, and believing in my story enough to challenge me and wait for me. You are an amazing woman! You have made the world a better place by your sacrifice and love for others. Thank you also for all of your time, energy and wisdom in editing for me. I am forever grateful!

Suzette Greer – Thank you for taking time to read my manuscript. You have encouraged me since the day we first shared our stories in the Wal-Mart parking lot. I appreciate our friendship and I look forward to the day that I read a Suzette Greer book!

Kortland Fuqua – Thank you for loving on us and walking alongside Doug and me, as we learned about marketing and speaking. Your knowledge and insight are invaluable to me. Thank you for your encouragement and confidence in me and my story.

Larry Nicholas, Nik Colyer, and Barry Carlos – Words cannot express my gratitude for your encouragement and support that you have all shared with me over the past year. You each have touched my heart in a meaningful way. Larry, I especially thank you and Shirley Barker Gillespie for leading me to my brother! Thank you all for your encouragement, wisdom, advice, and prayers!

Sandy Griffin – you were the very first person that I felt God lead me to and you confirmed the calling – thank you!

Ben Rait – Thank you for taking time to read my manuscript and encourage me to expand my words in certain chapters. Your input was valuable. Thank you. Now go write the book of your dreams!

To all of my friends, co-workers, neighbors, and family members, please forgive me for not calling you all by name but you know who you are... thank you for your prayers and encouragement. Thank you for inspiring me to stretch and grow. Thank you for being there for me when I needed you!

Introduction

As I sat on the front room couch with a blanket over me, I was watching the 10 o'clock news. I realized I was more tired than I thought I was. Normally I watch the local news and flip through various channels until I feel tired enough for sleep. I suddenly felt more than ready for bed, so I turned off the TV and went to my bedroom. I got into my bed, next to my sleeping husband, and laid my head on my pillow. I could feel myself ready for sleep. A few hours later, at 12:30am, I woke feeling very nauseous, disoriented, and wondered if I was suddenly coming down with the flu. I got up and went to the bathroom. As I stood up, my heart started racing wildly and I felt even more nauseous – and very afraid. My body was sweaty and clammy. My head was spinning. My chest was hurting. I slowly made it back to the bed after I realized I was not going to get sick. Maybe I just needed to lie down. For a brief moment I felt relief, then all of a sudden, waves of nausea hit me, such as I have never felt before. I felt a strong heat wave go through my body from my head to my toes. I felt my heart beating so fast that I thought it might beat out of my chest! I felt as if I could barely breathe. I was frantically trying to fill my lungs with air. I was very afraid. I felt like I was dying.

In February 2007, I was diagnosed with Anxiety, Panic, and Post Traumatic Stress Disorder. At first, I fought this diagnosis. I thought PTSD was only for people who served during wartime or who had some sort of major disaster happen in their life. I also did not believe that I had a panic attack. After my first attack, as I lay in the emergency room, I knew this was MUCH more serious than simply being anxious or worried. On that hospital bed, I knew there was something seriously wrong. I knew I was dying.

From all I have learned over the past few years this diagnosis is much more intricate and PTSD, panic and anxiety can go hand in hand. I realize now my diagnosis was correct. With God's strength, a supportive loving husband and children, as well as two amazing doctors, I am now on a path learning how to control and deal with my panic and anxiety. I am learning trigger points and how to use "the tools in my basket" to help me when situations come up that do trigger my anxious response. I am on a journey! For me I know this will be a life-long journey. I know there are many others who are also on a similar journey. Recognizing this fact has also helped me. It is important that we know that we are not alone. Our symptoms, triggers, and story may differ, but the underlining issue is the same.

I have felt like my life experiences have been a series of puzzle pieces. I did not know what the final puzzle would look like, but I knew that I needed to put the pieces together to bring order to my life. The goal of this book is to honestly examine each piece as an individual and with God's help, put them together.

This is not a book complaining about my childhood or being a victim. This book is **not** meant to tell **every** aspect of my life. The events, situations, and experiences I tell about are what I feel propelled me into PTSD, panic, and anxiety. It was not one event for me; it was a lifetime of events, circumstances, and people. As I look back I can see each of these situations and experiences as threads in my life, threads that are not necessarily strong on their own but woven together they created a cord that hung firmly from my neck. The threads, scarlet in color, signify the guilt and shame I felt over different situations and events in my life.

Some things that I mention are to show the patterns I was in that propelled me towards PTSD. I take full responsibility for the things I chose to do and for the relationships I chose to pursue and stay in. While I do not blame anyone or anything, you will see that I was primed for relationships and situations that plunged me into PTSD, panic and anxiety. You will see certain patterns emerge very early on for me. Perhaps you will be able to recognize patterns and situations in your life and make corrections earlier than I was able to. My heart's desire is to help someone who needs to hear my story.

As I began this journey of writing I was not sure why or exactly what would come of it. I just knew that I needed to do it. It was very evident to me as I got closer to the end, that God was showing me clearly He was there from the very beginning to the present time. The picture of this is all of the scriptures woven through each chapter. It was as if God was walking through this with me and very lovingly and gently proving Himself to me repeatedly.

At the end of each chapter, you'll find a section called **What I Know Now**. These concepts serve to give you some perspective into what I have learned since then or a spiritual truth that helped me along the way, as I was searching for hope. **There is always hope...**

Romans 15:4 "For whatever was written in earlier times was written for our instruction, so that through perseverance and the encouragement of the Scriptures we might have hope."

Puzzle Piece 1

The Beginning

Psalm 139:13-16

For You formed my inward parts; You wove me in my mother's womb. I will give thanks to You, for I am fearfully and wonderfully made; Wonderful are Your works, and my soul knows it very well. My frame was not hidden from You, when I was made in secret and skillfully wrought in the depths of the earth; Your eyes have seen my unformed substance. And in Your book were all written the days that were ordained for me, when as yet there was not one of them.

Sandy was eighteen years old and newly divorced from her first husband. She wanted a fresh start in life, and decided to move from Fairfield, California, back to Hayward, California. She moved in with her mom and younger sister, in a small two-bedroom apartment.

Russ was twenty-three years old and had recently returned home from his three-year commitment in the Navy. His high school sweetheart had broken up with him right before he returned. He was heartbroken but determined to move

1

forward. He had settled back into a routine of work and parties.

He and his friend Bob were roommates in the same apartment complex where Sandy lived with her mom. Russ and Sandy flirted with each other whenever their paths crossed in the parking lot or within the hallway of the apartment complex.

Sandy was attracted to Russ' soft blue eyes, light brown hair, and friendly smile. He was not a tall man, but at 5 foot 8 inches, he was 4 inches taller than she was. Russ was attracted to Sandy's long blonde hair, blue eyes, and her carefree ways.

They had been dating a few months when Sandy became pregnant. Russ' mother and father strongly encouraged a marriage commitment. Within a few weeks, Russ' parents planned and paid for a small simple wedding. The two of them drove to Reno, Nevada along with Russ' parents, grandparents and his younger sister. No one from Sandy's side of the family came.

Seven months later, Sandy and Russ welcomed me into their life. As a child, I know that my parents loved me and that I was well cared for. While my parents' marriage started out with hopes and dreams of a happy family life together, somewhere along the line those hopes and dreams were crushed. The end of their marriage was the beginning of my guilt and the threads that would later become part of my scarlet cord. At the tender age of five, I felt responsible for their feelings and for the demise of our family.

I do not have many early memories of my family life. However, I do remember my fifth birthday party. This was the last birthday we celebrated together. I remember the gift my parents gave me. It was a yellow electric car that I could sit on and drive. My dad was excited to give me this gift. He could hardly wait for me to see it. That day was one of the few good memories that I have.

I also have memories of them arguing and yelling at one another. One time my parents were in the kitchen and they began to argue; their voices were quickly escalating. I was in the front room watching TV. I glanced quickly towards the kitchen and a huge knot formed in my stomach. I could not see them, but I could hear the tone and the angry words coming from them. My dad told me to go and play in my room. I got up off the couch and headed to my room. I sat on my bed and someone closed my bedroom door. I heard them yelling and I heard crying. I grabbed my doll CiCi, and my favorite blanket. I held them both tightly to my chest. I felt scared and sad. I wanted my mom and dad to stop yelling at each other. I wanted to run out to the kitchen and hug them. I was not sure why they were fighting but I thought maybe I was somehow responsible or that I could make them stop. I was afraid to open my bedroom door and find out.

After five years of marriage, they both wanted out. By that time, they had both started drinking heavily, fighting, making accusations, and making life miserable for each other. While no one ever told me it was my fault, my five-year-old mind was thinking it had to be.

My mom decided to move to Santa Ana, California to live with her oldest sister and her family. I was in the middle of my kindergarten year; they agreed I would finish out the school year and continue to live with my dad. What happened after that is questionable. My dad said that before my mom moved out, she willingly signed legal documents giving him permanent custody of me. My mom says she signed the documents, but there was a verbal agreement between them stating that at the end of the school year she would have permanent custody of me, and I would move to Santa Ana to live with her. My dad says there was never a verbal agreement between them. My mom says my dad tricked her.

It was a difficult divorce filled with deceit and anger. In 1971, it was rare for the California Courts to hear a father's voice. As my dad fought to maintain custody of me, I felt torn, wanting to live with both parents.

My dad ultimately gained permanent custody of me. My mom was unhappy with the twice-yearly visitation and weekly phone contact that the judge awarded her. She continually took my dad back to court. She wanted more visitations and was hopeful she might gain permanent custody of me. The judge wanted to hear from me. The best way for that was through a Child Advocate Attorney.

As I sat across the table from a kind middle-aged woman, she asked me questions about my parents. The weight of the situation sat heavy on my heart. I was nervous trying to remember what both of my parents told me to say. I could not remember which parent had told me what, and all of the earlier insecurities of my first years came rushing back, making me feel that no matter what I said, it was going to be the wrong answer. I wanted to believe that I held a magic key to getting my family back together. I wanted to say the right things to make it all work.

Shortly after my parent's divorce was final, they each remarried – on the same day, in same state, and each bride was 'with child'. I am the 'only child' between Sandy and Russ – I am the oldest of six children in my dad's home. I am the oldest of two in my mom's home. Between the ages of six and fifteen, I grew up with my dad, stepmom, her two sons from a previous marriage, and three much younger half-siblings.

What I Know Now:

1. God purposed me to be born with the specific DNA of each of my parents. My parents may not have "planned" me, but God did. I was not an accident.
2. I was not responsible for my parents' arguments.
3. I was not responsible for the end of my parents' marriage.
4. It is natural for children of divorced parents to feel confused and want to live with both parents.
5. My parents (unintentionally) put me in the middle of their divorce and feelings for one another. This allowed guilt and shame to begin to take control.
6. In my opinion, counseling should always be required for children of divorced families. Divorce affects the whole family. Children and adults cope differently. Children do not have the emotional maturity or verbal communication skills to fully communicate what is going on inside of their hearts and minds. They often tell each parent what they think that parent wants to hear.
7. Communication from both parents to the child is vital, especially in reassuring the child that the divorce is not the child's fault.
8. Each year a million children are affected by divorce. (www.divorceandkids.com/divorce-statistics.htm)

Puzzle Piece 2

Shame and Guilt

John 14:27
*Peace I leave with you; My peace I give to you; not
as the world gives do I give to you. Do not let your
heart be troubled, nor let it be fearful.*

After many ugly court battles, my dad continued to retain
full legal custody of me. When I visited my mom on the twice-
yearly court-allotted visits, I felt sad and guilty when it was
time to say goodbye to her. I felt I was the cause of all her
tears and sadness. During our visits, my mom at times would
ask me to come and sit with her and talk. These conversations
always made me feel nervous. She would tell me many terrible
and disturbing things about my dad, things that a child could
never fully comprehend. She would also question me, and I
would frantically search my mind to give her the answers she
was looking for. These questions usually pertained to things
about her. "Sheryl, if you could change one thing about me,
what would it be?" I nervously answered that I wished she
would quit smoking – it seemed like the safest answer – and
she took a longer-than-normal drag on her cigarette as she

smiled at my stepdad and said, "Well, that just won't change," and the smile she shared with my stepdad gave me relief. I picked something that did not make her sad.

All too soon, each visit reached another ending. As we headed towards the airport, I knew that our relationship would be back to a short phone call on the weekends and the homemade cards she would send me in the mail. It would be six months before we would see each other again. On the way home, I would play back the picture of my mom in my mind, her long beautiful blonde hair, her makeup applied with perfection, even her smell; she frequently applied Rose Milk hand lotion, so she always smelled of roses. Her home was always nice, clean and had a loving feel. Beds always made, laundry always put away, ashtrays always emptied and cleaned at night, and cupboards were orderly, dishes never stayed in the sink, counters always clean and free of clutter. The coffee tables and shelves were always free of dust and the floors were always vacuumed, mopped, and swept. During meal times, we sat at the dinner table as a family. Despite the outward appearances, I still did not feel safe. I felt that I had to be constantly on guard. I was also still yearning for a life with her, and more than that, a life with her and my dad together again.

When I was home at my dad's he would tell me things like "your momma just ain't right." He would also make demeaning comments about my stepdad and call him names. I never liked this but I never said anything. One day, my dad told me that my mom had been married before she married him. He also told me that she had a baby boy that she had abandoned before she met him. He told me his name was LeRoy. I did not want to believe my dad. I knew he had to be making that up. I soon found out it was true. During one summer visit, my mom and stepdad said they had something very important to tell me. They proceeded to tell me I had an older brother. His name is LeRoy. I felt guilty and ashamed that I already knew this information. I felt remorseful that I did not want to believe my dad. I suddenly felt jealous of my "new" brother. I wondered if he would get to see my mom more than I did. I wondered if he would get to live with her. At age 13, he was three years older than I was. I was surprised at how tall he was, and unlike the blonde hair that I shared with my mom, his was brown. His eyes were also brown, not blue like my mom's or green like mine. He seemed to be a typical teenage boy. He listened to hard rock music. He liked to joke around a lot and was playful and kind to our younger sister and me. I did not know a whole lot about him or the situation. He was suddenly a part of my life and then without warning he was gone from my life again. He was no longer there when I went for visits any more. No one mentioned him or his family again. I never questioned this, as I knew it would be best not to ask any questions. I did not want to be the cause of making anyone sad or angry by questioning what was going on.

The short visits I had with my mom always included fun trips, new clothes, and quality time. My mom always made sure that we went somewhere fun. There were many trips to Disneyland, Knotts Berry Farm, parks, and fairs. They made sure I left with more clothes than I came with. We also enjoyed playing many games together. One of my favorites, at that time, was The Peanut Butter and Jelly board game. I loved that game. I frequently cheated to ensure my mom or I won, while my stepdad was always the loser. At my request, they also played house and doctor with me. Usually, I had my mom and I play the mother and daughter roles, while I made my stepdad be the stranger or the bad person. Whenever I got out the doctor kit, I was always the doctor and my mom was always the nurse, while my stepdad was the sick patient. It never failed that whatever ailed him, Dr. Sheryl had to give him a shot, sometimes more than one. I always had to make sure that the injection went firmly into his arm. He was always a brave patient and had a smile on his face. Looking back, I know that I was influenced by my dad's comments and feelings about my stepdad and unfortunately, I was not always very kind to him. I was not a competitive person so it was not that I had to win the games we played, I just did not want "him" to win. In spite of it all, he still loved me. He seemed to understand the reasons I was responding to him that way was because of my situation. He was the only person I ever treated this way.

As I mentioned, our visits together were always fun, with the exception of the last few days. Those were spent in quiet sadness. The reality of not seeing each other for months on end was hard for all of us. During one particular visit, as our time was ending, my mom and stepdad asked me if I wanted to live with them. Of course, I said yes! The rest of the day our conversations revolved around the possibility of us moving, changing our names and never ever seeing my dad, grandparents, or other family again. I cried when I began to understand all the implications. As my mom and stepdad recorded the conversation, I called my dad and told him that I was not coming home. I began crying harder. I could not bear not seeing him or my family again! The next thing I knew my dad was at the front door with a Sheriff. My mom calmly gathered all my things and put them in my suitcase. She hugged me and with tears in her eyes, she told me not to ever forget how much she loves me. As my dad and I got into the car, we both cried and hugged one another. We rode to the airport in the back of the Sheriff's car. I felt responsible for the pain and anguish that I saw in my dad and for the tears and heartache I saw in my mom. I felt all of this was my fault, and I cried the entire flight home. The threads of my scarlet cord were beginning to get a little bit thicker.

Once we got home, no one ever spoke of this incident again. For reasons unknown to me, my dad chose not to file charges against my mom. I struggled internally with my feelings of guilt for wanting to live with my mom, and for saying yes to their plan even though once I realized what it meant, I did not want it. I felt guilt for telling my dad I did not want to come home when I knew he wanted me to come home. I felt fear and guilt when I saw the Sheriff at the door. In my child's mind, the police and sheriff only come to get the "bad guys." I felt I must have been bad since a sheriff came to get me and take me home. I had no way of communicating what was going on inside my mind and heart. I did not have the words to express myself. There was not any type of communication afterward. The whole situation was pushed under the rug and never brought up again. Sweeping things under the rug and not talking about them anymore continued as a lifelong pattern and ultimately lead to my first panic attack.

What I Know Now:

1. Children are not responsible for the emotions that their parents experience due to the consequences of their parents' actions or choices.

2. Parents should reserve their opinions and negative stories about one another for other adults, not their children. Sharing these opinions inappropriately almost always has a damaging affect on the children.

3. Parents should never try to take court orders into their own hands. Doing so places children in situations in which they are predisposed to guilt. In the extreme situation where a child may be in danger, immediately seek legal or professional advice, contacting either the police or the local child abuse hotline.

4. Never allow yourself to sweep things under the rug, no matter how difficult the situation is. Age appropriate communication is vital. Not talking about a situation doesn't make it go away.

5. Children should not be the confidant for their parents' secrets or feelings. Children are unable to process such things on an adult level. This creates a huge burden for them and sets them up for shame and guilt.

Puzzle Piece 3

My New Family

Psalm 34:18-19
The LORD is near to the brokenhearted, and saves those who are crushed in spirit.

Although my dad and my stepmom did try to make us a family, I still longed for my mom. I wanted "my" family back. My dad felt things would come more natural in our new family if I started calling my stepmom "mom." I did not want to do this. It's not that I hated my stepmom, I didn't. She could have been Carol Brady or June Cleaver, but she was not "*my* mom." I felt that I had my own mom and I did not need another one, plus I was still hopeful that someday my parents would reconcile. Even though both my parents had made it crystal clear this would never happen, I still had hope. My dad took me for several car rides to try to talk me into calling his new wife "mom." After all the car trips, (guilt trips), I finally said it. "Mom." One little word seemed to make everyone happy – everyone but me. Saying and doing things to make others happy at my own expense developed into a pattern of behavior that set me up for an abusive marriage.

I was very close to my three youngest siblings, I was definitely a second mom to them. This was not forced on me. I willingly took on the role, and my stepmom freely let me. As much as I wanted to be the only child, I also loved being needed and wanted by my siblings. There was not much fighting or sibling rivalry between any of us kids. We all got along and we were protective of each other. It would be a rare time when one of the youngest was not with me in my bed at night. This innocent family routine came back later to haunt me in my first marriage.

As a family, we always seemed to be struggling financially. This was difficult for me to accept, since no child wants to be 'less than' when compared with their peers. We were told to tell the cashier at the local store "please hold this check for a week." And they always did. They knew us and knew our story. I was so aware of this that I would walk around the store until I was sure no one I knew was at the checkout. Many times, we qualified for free lunch at school. With the exception of the new clothes that my mom bought during our visits, I always wore hand-me-downs. Our home and vehicles always looked unsightly and impoverished. Many times we were on welfare and received food stamps. With six kids, two adults and the "extra" kids that my stepmom took in to make a little extra income babysitting, our home was always chaotic and unkempt. No one really cared about outward appearances there. We all did what we had to do to get to the next day.

There was nothing significant about our home life. Our home just was. We lived in a middle class neighborhood in a three bedroom, one bathroom home. The house had blue carpet, and it was furnished with hand-me-down furniture. My dad's parents gave my dad and stepmom money to buy new front room curtains. My stepmom chose red sheers that had a bold black and white print curtain that went over the red sheers. My grandmother hated the new curtains that my stepmom picked out. My stepmom and my grandmother's styles and ideas seemed to clash quite often. My dad's parents rarely came to our home. Holidays were a rare time when my stepmom and all the kids were invited to go to my grandparent's home.

As children, we had many chores to do. It seemed our dryer was always broken, so it was my job to hang all of the laundry outside on the clothesline. With eight people in the family, there was always lots of laundry to do. If I left it out there too many days, pincher bugs seemed to invade the clean clothes on the line. I hated these bugs and the way the laundry always felt so stiff and scratchy from the sun and wind drying them out. While dusting, vacuuming, and emptying ashtrays were never a priority in our home, dirty dishes were. My two stepbrothers and I had to take turns washing dishes every night. As I look back, our kitchen was still always dirty. It also seemed that I had to wash a clean cup if I wanted something to drink, as we never really washed the dishes very well in the first place. It was not required of us to make our beds as long as things were picked up off the floor at night, it didn't matter if we shoved things under the beds or in the closets.

Having one bathroom with eight people at times made life stressful. The door did not have a lock on it, so unless you pulled the drawer from the bathroom counter out, as a way to block the door from opening, privacy was never guaranteed. There were rough scratchy towels we had to use for our showers and baths, and the smell of urine was also constant in the bathroom.

Dinner times at our home were always quick and quiet. The kids sat at the kitchen table and my dad and stepmom ate in the front room. This made it easy when we had things on our dinner plate that we did not like. We would simply toss the food on the floor, under the table, and if we had a dog, as we often did, we let that dog in briefly to clean our floor. I did this a lot, especially when my stepmom made her favorite, liver and onions, for dinner.

Even though there was nothing abusive or detrimental in our home, I still yearned for the return of my 'ideal' family – my life before my parents' divorce. I did not let go of my child-like fantasy pretending that my parents might someday love one another again. I also deeply craved an emotional relationship with my dad. I knew that something was missing. The only time we ever connected was when he and I would visit his parents. Away from the distractions of all the other kids, my dad would talk to me, connect with me and I looked forward to those visits. One night I was brave enough to ask my dad if we could leave. I asked him if he and I could live with his parents. He looked at me with tears in his eyes and said, "Sheryl I can't just leave these other kids, we just got to stay." We did stay and I never asked again.

As I grew older, I dealt with this disconnect with my dad by pursuing unhealthy relationships, my dad dealt with his feelings by drinking. Since I felt that I had no one to share with, I kept my feelings and thoughts to myself. I was silently crying out for love and for the relationship I had with my dad when we were **not** at home.

As my childhood went on, I continued to add to the weight of guilt that I was carrying which added to the weight of my scarlet cord. I not only felt guilty for my parent's divorce, but also I felt guilty about certain privileges that none of the other children in the family had. I had visitation with my mom twice a year as well as weekly phone calls. I felt this made my stepbrothers sad, as their father did not have much contact with them during those years. Another privilege that I had was that I was the only child invited to spend weekends at my grandparents' or my aunt's home. Again I felt conflicted, since I had a longing to be with them, but I also knew it hurt my stepmom that the others were never invited. I often felt she resented me, but to her credit, she never treated me any differently.

Being at other family members' homes gave me a chance to be a kid, not the oldest of six and the second mother I had become. It gave me rare and special moments with my dad. We would talk and laugh about things, unlike when we were at home. When we were at home we rarely spoke to one another. He seldom spoke to anyone at all unless he was drinking with a friend. Away from home, he shared stories with me about his high school days, his friends, and his first true love. I took these stories in and held on to them tightly. I always felt safe in those moments. I felt special that my dad was sharing these things with me – I only wished it had been the 'norm' and not the exception.

What I Know Now:

1. Parents should not coerce their children into feeling something that they do not feel. Parents should never guilt a child into a decision. Clear communication is the best way to deal with all situations. As the adult, you need to make the right decision for your child, but it is also important that you hear your child's heart and consider all costs before you enforce something that is important to you.

2. Open communication is important in any relationship but much more so with blended families. These families are not only dealing with the realities of divorce but also the concepts of blending two different families into one.

3. Shame gives you a feeling that says *I am bad.* Guilt gives you the feeling *you did something bad.* Both of these feelings are healthy and needed in order to point us to repentance and change, but it's important to have a good balance. I did not have a good balance.

4. If you are struggling with guilt and shame, it is important that you find the root of the problem and deal with it. It is also important to forgive yourself (and others). Romans 8:1 tell us "There is no condemnation for those who are in Christ." If you have accepted Christ in your heart, there is no longer any reason to let guilt and shame control you. I once heard Liz Curtis Higgs say at a Women's Retreat, "You can not out sin God's mercy." Amen!

Puzzle Piece 4

From Generation to Generation

Hebrews 13:5
... for He Himself has said, "I will never desert you,
nor will I ever forsake you"

I am from a long line of alcoholics. Both of my parents are alcoholics. I know that both sets of grandparents were also alcoholics. I am sure the line goes even farther back on both sides. I never heard my dad's parents argue, become violent or aggressive towards one another or anyone for that matter. I never saw them stumble or passed out. This does not mean these things did not happen. I was simply not aware of them. My dad's parents showered me with love and affection whenever I was with them. When I spent weekends with them, I looked forward to the weekly trip my grandfather made to the local liquor store. I loved going with him because I always knew he would buy me a candy bar along with the usual order of two large bottles of alcohol. I never saw any outward signs of my grandparents being drunk but I cannot remember a time when I did not see a drink on either of my grandparent's coasters.

I have heard stories about my mom's mom and her wild drunken behavior. She suffered a serious medical condition by the time I was born and her drunken party days were over. The stories I heard from many family members never matched the grandma I knew. Although I never spent much quality time with her, the times we did spend together were always filled with talk of soap operas and the delicious food she made. The visits we had were always short and sweet. I do not know if she ever chose to believe and accept Jesus Christ before her death. We never shared any deep conversations.

Anything related to God, church, (even simple prayers) was absent in both my parents' homes. At times, I have questioned where God was in all this. Was He ever invited into either home? I do know there are some church roots in my dad's family. A few years ago, I was given a special book that a family member spent countless hours completing. It was filled with information and history about my dad's family, and dated back hundreds of years. Among the many interesting facts, I was surprised that there were preachers in our family. Religion seemed to play a significant role in a few of my relatives' lives. Somewhere in our bloodline, there were praying believers.

The one Bible I was given was from my mom and stepdad. Even though they gave me a Bible, faith and religion were not part of their daily life, either. My mom and stepdad visited the church that I accepted Christ in (when I was sixteen) for a short time. They suddenly stopped visiting because they felt someone in the church was being hypocritical. Sadly, my mom and stepdad always seemed to have a problem with the *people* in the church and never fully met the *God* of the church, though they still allowed my sister and me to attend. I know that my mom believes that there is a God and that He has a son named Jesus. I have talked with her and prayed with her on many occasions. My stepdad has dabbled in many religions and has a belief that all roads led to God. He and I have had many deep conversations on this topic. We agree to disagree.

I know now that Christ lives in my heart and I know that He has had his hand on me from birth – even if church and other things were not a part of my growing up. I can clearly recall a time before my parents' divorce when I was taking a bath and I was suddenly very aware of God at that moment. I remember feeling in awe and peaceful. At that moment, I knew that God **is** real, even though I had never been taken to church and no one had ever prayed with me. The next time I remember *feeling God* was later when I was living with my dad and stepmom. A bus would come into our neighborhood to pick up kids and take them to church. I do not recall how often we went or how long we continued to go. What I do recall is how Norm and his wife Judy would drive the bus around different neighborhoods and pick up as many kids as they could carry (with parental permission) and take us to the local Baptist church. I heard Bible stories and sang songs. I wanted to understand, but I did not have any foundations to build on. The only scripture I remember memorizing was John 3:16: "For God so loved the world that He gave His only begotten Son, that whosoever believes in Him shall not perish, but have eternal life." I know now that Norm, his wife Judy, and the Sunday School teachers planted seeds in me, seeds that did not sprout for many years to come.

What I Know Now:

1. An estimated 43% of US adults have had someone related to them who is presently, or was, an alcoholic. (www.treatment-centers.net/alcoholism.statistics.html)

2. There are 6 million minors in the US living with an alcoholic father or mother. (www.treatment-centers.net/alcoholism.statistics.html)

3. If you do not know of any praying believers in your family lineage, you can become the first. It's never too late to start praying for your family.

4. As believers in Christ, you are not bound by generational sins and curses from your parents or ancestors. We have a choice. We are responsible for our own behavior and choices. Through the life, death, and resurrection of Christ, we are no longer bound by generational sins and curses. Christ paid the ultimate price for our freedom to choose. While parents can influence how children may choose to live their lives, it is still about choices. The Bible tells us in II Corinthians 5:17 "Therefore if any man is in Christ, he is a **new** creature; the old things have passed away; behold, new things have come." You are no longer held in bondage to generational sins and curses. You have a choice. Grab it with both hands and hold tightly to God's promises.

Puzzle Piece 5

My Teen Years and Life at My Mom's

Ephesians 2:4-5
God, being rich in mercy, because of His great love
with which He loved us, even when we were dead in
our transgressions, made us alive together with
Christ, by whose grace you have been saved.

Life changed a lot for me the summer before the ninth grade. I began to get a lot of attention from boys. I liked the attention. I was longing for a relationship with someone. Unfortunately, a few boys in high school were all too eager to show me the affection and attention I was looking for, for all the wrong reasons. I began falling into "secret" patterns. I was willing to have a "secret" relationship with the football player or the popular guy in class. It was secret because either they had a girlfriend at the time or they did not act like a boyfriend around me while we were at school. They would not hold my hand down the hall, they were not interested in getting to know me for who I was, while at school. However, when they called me on the phone or the very rare times we were alone, then they would act as if they wanted me for a girlfriend. They would suddenly become very interested in me. My heart always hoped though that somehow they would open their eyes and say, "Sheryl, I love YOU! You are the one I want and need." That never happened. I was an easy target, so I do not blame those high school boys. I was willing **only** because I was hopeful. Looking back on this I remember a quote from one of my favorite movies, *That Thing You Do.* In the scene, the main girl character has just opened her eyes and heart to the awful truth of her boyfriend's true character and how he has treated her. She is brave enough to see it, acknowledge it, and move away from it, as she tells him, "I wasted too many kisses on you." I, too, was wasting too many kisses on undeserving young men.

I had a few non-secret relationships but they did not last long. Usually I broke up with the boy because I was still feeling the void in my heart. My first serious relationship was with a boy in my graduating class named Richard. We started dating October 1980 during my freshman year. While he had a "party" reputation, he did seem to fill my need for attention and love, though I also had to compete with his need for drugs and alcohol.

During the middle of my sophomore year in high school, I made a decision that devastated my dad and grandparents. I asked to live with my mom and stepdad. I will never forget the tears in my grandfather's eyes as he asked me why I wanted to leave and live with my mom. With tear-filled eyes, I answered very softly, "I don't know, I just want to." I did not know how to tell him truthfully that I had wanted out for a long time. I was tired of the endless responsibilities of babysitting and chores. I saw life at my mom's as an escape. For the most part each visit with her was always filled with quality time, gifts, and fun. I also knew she wanted me to live with her. I knew if I lived with her, she would no longer be sad because I would be coming "home" to her.

This was the first time that my dad refused to talk to me. After the initial conversation, he refused to talk to me for over a year. Even though I was excited that I was going to have my dream of living with my mom, I felt my words and desires were reprehensible in my dad's eyes. The guilt I felt over this decision only added to the weight of the threads that were now officially a scarlet cord, as it sat invisibly around my neck.

From age fifteen to eighteen, I lived with my mom, stepdad, and younger sister. Life at my mom and stepdad's was very different from my dad's. Having only one sibling in the house made a lot of difference. I did not have the responsibilities that I had at my dad's house. Things were always quiet and the house was always clean. Money was not an issue there. No hand-me-downs, no free lunch line, no food stamps. Things were clean, orderly, and looked good from the outside. Appearances mattered there.

Shortly after moving in with my mom, I found out I was pregnant. I was fifteen years old. I honestly had no idea I was pregnant. I was so foolish and naïve to think I could have unprotected sex and not get pregnant. My boyfriend Richard and I had been dating for a year before I moved in with my mom. We started having sex within a few months of dating.

My mom intended to educate me on sex, but not from a Biblical or moral standpoint. When I was in middle school, my mom sat me down for "the talk" during a weekend visit. She told me "sex was good and natural." She offered to show me photos of naked men. I was embarrassed and uncomfortable and told her "no." She never talked about protection, waiting until marriage, diseases, or pregnancy. It seemed as if her only concern was for me to recognize that sex is normal, it is good, and that I could come to her at any time with questions. I was embarrassed to ask her questions, and honestly, I didn't know what to question, I just listened. There were not any other adults in my life who talked so openly about sex. With the exception of physical body development, the school system, at the time, did not teach on the subject at all. It was similar to the "don't ask-don't tell" philosophy.

My boyfriend and I did not use protection. We never talked about the need for protection or the possibility of pregnancy. My mom was very angry when she found out I was sexually active. She was not angry I was *having* sex, she was angry I did not *tell* her I was. She had expected me to be as open with her as she was with me.

The truth of my actions only became known because she found out from the high school attendance office that I had cut school, so the next day she came home early and went through all of my things. She and my step dad suspected I was doing drugs. I was not. My friend Kim and I had cut school to go to The Eden Youth Center, which is similar to a Planned Parenthood facility. My friend was also sexually active and wanted to get birth control pills without her mother's consent. I thought it would probably be good for me to get on birth control pills as well. I did not want to talk with my mom about this. I hid the pills and the condoms I received from the clinic in my jewelry box. My jewelry box had a small lock on the front. I did not intentionally lock the box but some how it locked. Once my mom and stepdad noticed it was locked they knew something must have been in there that I was hiding. They, of course, were right; it just was not what they had suspected.

My mom was furious and hurt that I had lied to her when she had asked me if I was a virgin and if I was sexually active the day I moved in with them. At the time, I told her I was a virgin and I was not sexually active. I did not want her to know the truth about me. I felt ashamed. Most of my close friends were not sexually active, and the friends that I had that were sexually active had a wild reputation. I did not want "that" reputation. I did not want anyone to think badly of me. Even though my mom did her best to talk to me at an early age about sex, something inside of me felt it was wrong. I was uncomfortable talking so openly about this with her. I feared that if she knew the truth about me then she might not love me anymore. She might regret letting me move in with her.

After my mom found the birth control pills and condoms, she insisted that I have a full gynecological exam with her doctor. This included a pregnancy test. A few days later, we received a call from the doctor's office. The nurse asked to speak to me. After I said hello, the nurse said, "Sheryl, your pregnancy test is positive." At that very moment, I felt ashamed and sad. I cried. I did not want to get off the phone and have to tell my mom and stepdad the news. My mom immediately told me that there was no other option except abortion. I knew I wanted my baby even though I had no idea what being a parent really meant. My mom made it clear they would not help me support or raise a baby; if I kept the baby, I would have to go back to my dad's house. She also conveyed how mad and disappointed my dad would be. My mom believed my dad would have never supported me with a baby. My boyfriend's parents *may* have supported me, but their oldest son's girlfriend was also pregnant. I think they were just relieved that I would go through with an abortion. I felt I did not have a choice, so I reluctantly went. I was taken to a doctor who put me to sleep for the procedure. I was crying as they put the mask over my face. I wanted to scream "NO!" but I did not.

Once we returned home things went back to "normal." Once again a situation was swept under the rug, and no one ever talked about what happened again. This situation made the weight of my scarlet cord begin to feel the heaviest it had ever felt. My boyfriend and I continued in our relationship but in an off-and-on-again dependency. Neither one of us ever brought up the subject of pregnancy or abortion again. Now that we no longer lived in the same city, the time we spent together was limited. When we were "off," I slipped so easily back into the patterns of seeking out unhealthy, sometimes-secretive relationships. I wanted to be someone else but I did not know how. The weight of my guilt and shame seemed to smother me. I felt so stuck in my patterns that I just kept going. Even though I had started attending church, I felt like I could not connect the two sides of me. One half desired all that I heard Jesus offers, and the other half bore all of my condemnation, insecurities and low self esteem. I could not connect the two. Grace was right in front of me but I felt too unworthy to grab it with both hands.

During my last two years of high school, I developed two groups of friends. I had church friends and non-church friends. My non-church friends did not know anything about my acceptance of Christ, my baptism, or anything related to that side of me. My church friends had no idea that I had a completely different life away from them. The church I started attending, Peninsula Bible Church in Palo Alto, California, was the one that my little sister was attending at the time. Each Sunday morning Pastor Herman Shaw would drive the bus around town and pick up anyone who wanted to come to church. I came to accept Christ and I was baptized there. I really liked the youth pastor and his wife. I saw something in Pastor Mike and his wife Leana's life, something between them that I had not seen before. I could not pin point what it was but I was drawn to it. I went on a few excursions and weekend retreats with the youth group. I saw Amy Grant at a local amusement park. I was overwhelmed at how many "perfect" people I saw at her concert. I was sure no one there ever walked in the shoes that I was walking in. I listened to Amy Grant and David Meece constantly on my cassette player. I truly desired to change the patterns I was in but I lacked the tools and the foundation to change these behaviors. This led to another unhealthy relationship. My boyfriend and I were starting to drift apart more and more. The distance was affecting our relationship. After being together for almost two years, during my junior year in high school, we broke up for the last time. I was sad, but at the same time I felt like I needed to move forward with people who didn't know about my past or my abortion. I had two friends who were sisters, who went to my school and the church I was attending. They had an older brother who had already graduated high school. We started dating and before I knew it the relationship turned sexual. We hid that aspect of our relationship from everyone, living a lie. Going to church and retreats but also continuing to open doors that God ordained only for a husband and wife. That relationship lasted less than a year but all of the guilt and shame I felt having it added to the weight of my scarlet cord, and inside I continued to feel ashamed and worthless.

I mentally fought with myself time and time again. I desperately wanted to be someone who stood for something. I wanted to be strong but felt so weak. I wanted that unconditional love and acceptance, I yearned for a clean slate and forgiveness. I also had a very unhealthy mindset that it was my responsibility to make others happy. I was struggling with low self-esteem. It was hard to imagine that Jesus could **really** love me that much and care about me **that much**. All I really knew at that time was I was very unworthy.

What I Know Now:

1. I was looking for an emotional connection. I was willing to sacrifice my needs or desires if I thought someone loved me.

2. I had an unhealthy view of relationships and boundaries.

3. One of the reasons I felt that my first serious relationship *seemed* to fill all of my voids was because it fit the patterns I was use to. My boyfriend's drug and alcohol use kept us from getting too close and I subconsciously thought that I could help him.

4. No one **needs** a relationship, outside of Christ, in order to be complete in life.

5. According to the Guttmacher Institute, in the year 2003 alone, there were almost 1.3 million abortions performed.

6. The affects from abortion are life long. Unfortunately, forgiveness does not come with an eraser.

7. There are other options besides abortion. Today there are many resources available to help you if you decide to keep your baby or want to consider adoption.

8. The one redeeming fact that I hold onto is that I know my baby is in Heaven. An aborted baby is not any different from a baby that has been miscarried or stillborn, I believe they go straight into the arms of Jesus. I know now that I am forgiven and I accept that, but I will always regret having an abortion. Someday I look forward to holding my baby in Heaven.

9. There is no such thing as a perfect Christian. Jesus isn't looking for you to get all cleaned up and figure things out before you come to Him. He wants you just as you are.

Puzzle Piece 6

And then came marriage

I Corinthians 13:4-7

Love is patient, love is kind and is not jealous; love does not brag and is not arrogant, does not act unbecomingly; it does not seek its own, is not provoked, does not take into account a wrong suffered, does not rejoice in unrighteousness, but rejoices with the truth; bears all things, believes all things, hopes all things, endures all things.

The beginning of my senior year of high school, I was not dating anyone until I met a guy who went to my school. His name and reputation were well known on campus. I knew he had a temper and I knew he liked to party. One evening he came into the store where I was working and while I was helping him locate an item, we started talking. One thing led to another and he came back after I was off work. I was flattered. He pursued and I followed. I thought I could love him, care for him, help him, and change him. I wanted to believe all the things that love was suppose to be and that love never fails. This relationship tested those beliefs for the next nine years. We started dating exclusively from the very beginning. He was charming and attentive. He always wanted to be around me and know what I was doing. He was interested in me. At the time, I felt very special that he wanted to spend so much time with me. We had only been dating a few short months when he asked me to marry him on Christmas Day in 1983. I said yes, even though I knew he had already proposed to two other girls over the past two years. I was seventeen and he was eighteen. We had previously talked about marriage but I did not think engagement would be so soon. I was thrilled at the thought of being someone's wife but also apprehensive about what marriage really meant.

Parents at times are considered the enemy whenever they try to 'interfere' with their child's love life, but there was a part of me that wanted my mom and stepdad to question us, to step in and make us wait. I wanted them to ask us the hard questions and see if we were ready for such a life-changing decision. However, there were no questions. They said they were happy for us and we moved forward.

While I do not feel that my mom and stepdad acted very 'parental' in many areas of my life, they did have a plan should anyone in the family get in trouble or need immediate help. They created a code word, a simple number, that would tell the other family member **I need you, there is something wrong**. This word would alert my stepdad if my mom, my sister, or I were in a situation that we were unable to communicate that we needed help or rescuing. The word could easily fit into an every day kind of sentence, but it would alert my stepdad that there was a big problem and his help was vital. I do not know how long they had this word nor how it came about. To my knowledge, I am the only one in the family who has ever used it.

Shortly after our engagement, I had to use the code word for the first time in my life. I had gone to see my fiancé at the room he was renting while on a break between my classes. No one else was at the house. I did not intend to skip the rest of the school day. I only wanted to stop by and say hi. I ended up staying there until after 6:00 pm. He had been drunk since the night before, and continued to drink while I was there. Even though I had a lot of exposure within my family to those who were drunk, this was the first time I experienced fear from the effect the alcohol was having on someone. I had never experienced physical danger from a drunken person until that day. I was filled with fear. He showed me a gun and told me he could shoot people and kill them, including me if he wanted. I was so frightened that I had no idea if I was going to die that day or not. I felt like a prisoner. At one point, the UPS man came to the door to deliver a package for the owner of the home. I wanted to slip him a note, but there was no way I could do it without being caught. He was out of control. He seemed to vacillate between anger and tears. He did not have one specific issue; everything was a target of his rage. At one point he got very angry with me, took my engagement ring off, said that I did not deserve it and proceeded to swallow it! At that moment, I prayed in my head for God to protect me and to let me get out of there alive. I felt frozen in time. I did not feel that I could leave when I wanted. Mixed in with the fear I also felt sad for him. It was obvious he had many issues. I had no idea exactly what they were, and I felt powerless to help him. I tried to comfort him and assure him of my love. I wanted to show him that I did deserve his love and his ring. He began to cry and said he knew I must not love him anymore. I felt like I was in a dream. I had never been around anyone who acted like this. I felt compassion and fear all at the same time. I believed he had the ability to do all the violent things he said he could. I also loved him and wanted to help him.

At another point, he stopped drinking and seemed to be sobering up a little. I knew I needed to leave but I also knew I needed a good reason that he would believe and be agreeable to. I told him, "I need to check in with my parents. They are probably worried about me as it is now dinnertime, and I am supposed to help make dinner." He allowed me to call them. As soon as my stepdad answered, I used the code word in a sentence that I knew he would understand. I told my stepdad that I needed a certain number of eggs to make the meatloaf I promised to make for dinner that night. They were not expecting me to make dinner that night and by that time they had already eaten dinner. Suddenly my stepdad realized I was using the code word. Once he confirmed my use of the word, he promised to come immediately. He did. Once he arrived, he walked in the house and said, "Sheryl needs to come home now." I was allowed to leave. My stepdad followed me home in his car. Once I was home, as soon as I walked in, I realized my mom had also been drinking. This meant she would soon be angry about something or someone. I ran to my room crying. I was scared and felt completely alone. I did not know what to do. I kept playing the entire day over and over in my head asking myself what could I have done differently, what did I say to trigger his anger towards me? Did I deserve his ring? The tears he shed seemed to make me feel that deep down he was sorry and did not really mean all the things he had said and done. I felt alone, confused, and guilty.

Within an hour, he called me. He told me he wanted to give me the ring back (he obviously did not really swallow it). He also told me how much he loved me and needed me. He said I was the best thing in the world for him. He said he wanted to be with me. Since I felt that his outburst must have been my fault, I was very anxious to return to him and fix it. I bravely went downstairs and told my mom, "he called, he needs me, and I need to go get him so we can work this out." She did not stop me. She did not question me. I was relieved that she agreed and that whatever she was mad about that time seemed to have nothing to do with me. Deep in my heart, I was surprised that neither my mom nor my stepdad seemed concerned that I had just used our most secret family code word to be rescued. I left and that was the beginning of my journey deeper into PTSD.

Looking back on this puzzle piece, my fiancé never apologized, he never took responsibility for his actions or his drinking, and he never acknowledged the fear he put in me, or that he had done anything "wrong." I felt that somehow I must have done something to trigger him otherwise he would have not have become angry with me and taken my ring. He always wanted to blame me for his choices. I know now that you cannot make rational sense out of another person's irrational behavior, nor was I responsible for his choices or his behavior.

A few months after my mom and stepdad rescued me from my abusive fiancé, they wanted to look for a smaller less expensive place to live. Since I was engaged, they encouraged us to live together. I think we were both a little apprehensive at first. The reality of our own apartment seemed a little overwhelming. In the end, we decided to do it since we were already spending so much time together. My fiancé was having a hard time getting and keeping an apartment on his own. He stayed with us sometimes for weeks at a time when he did not have a place to go. I continued to let his problems become mine. With my mom and stepdad's help, we got our first apartment together in the spring of 1984. We furnished it with several items I already had, and my mom and stepdad bought a couch, chair, TV, and a dining room table for us from local garage sales they frequented. While I suddenly felt very grown up moving in with my boyfriend, I was also aware that my dad would not approve of this. Again, I struggled with feelings of shame and guilt. Things seemed to be moving too fast. I knew that I did not want my dad to know I was living with my boyfriend. I was not worried about what my friends might have thought, as by this time most of my friends had slowly disappeared from my daily life. Our relationship was so exclusive that I rarely had time for any other socializing or girlfriend time. Any time I spent with a friend he was always there; he was a part of everything in my life. My world seemed to get smaller and smaller as we got closer and closer.

Shortly after we moved into our first apartment, my mom and stepdad told us they were going to go to Reno, Nevada in a few weeks. If we went with them they would pay for everything, including a limo, if we wanted to go ahead and get married at that time. They were not sure they would be able to make the same offer in August, which is when we had talked about setting a wedding date. I felt torn, as my dad was not speaking to me because I had done something to disappoint him again. I had always dreamed of a wedding with my dad walking me down the aisle. I was also not sure, if he *had* been speaking to me, that he would have approved of my marriage. I decided not to tell him until afterward. I was relieved that I would not have to hide the fact I was living with my boyfriend anymore – I would be married.

In my heart, I was hopeful that marriage might make life better for us. My soon-to-be husband was always questioning my love for him, always jealous of my past relationships. Saying my vows to him would prove once and for all my love and loyalty to him. I also think we were both looking at marriage as the answer to all the issues each of us had: loss, heartache, emptiness, shame, guilt, and disappointment. Both of us, at a very young age, dreamed of being married to someone, as if that held a magic key towards healing and wholeness. Deep down I was also fighting within myself. I felt that this was not God's plan for my life. It was *my* plan and I continued to march forward. I chose to ignore my feelings. We would be man and wife. I said my vows and I vowed to make it work forever and to be the best wife I could. We were married on May 27, 1984. Several weeks later, I graduated high school. Many people at school (peers and teachers) asked if I was pregnant. I said no, but secretly I wished I was.

What I Know Now:

1. As a parent, I am proactive in all aspects of the lives of my children. If I see red flags in any relationship they may have, I have and will continue to question and talk openly with them.

2. Red flags usually stay the same color.

3. I am not responsible for other people's choices, their pasts, or their issues.

4. While establishing a code word in case of emergency is a great idea, if a family member uses it, make sure to talk about every aspect of why the word was used in the first place. Recognize the signs of an abusive relationship, and help that person by talking and listening without judging. Encourage that person to put up healthy boundaries and to seek additional help via counseling or if necessary law enforcement.

5. You should **never** feel fear in any relationship.

6. Make sure you marry for the right reasons. You should never marry in the hopes of changing someone, proving your love and loyalty to them, because of pressure from circumstances or people, or because you are looking for that person to rescue you from any negative feelings you may feel in your own life.

Puzzle Piece 7

The Beating

Psalm 56:3-4

When I am afraid, I will put my trust in You. In God, whose word I praise, In God I have put my trust; I shall not be afraid. What can mere man do to me?

Just months after using the secret family code word to be rescued from my abusive fiancé, I needed to use the word again to be rescued from my abusive husband. My husband and I had gone to a friend's house for a party. Everyone was over 21 except the two of us. I was not drinking. He was. As he got drunker by the minute, I was beginning to feel anxious about the situation. I realized when he reached a certain point in his drinking he would become verbally abusive, very physical, and very angry. He was quickly getting to that point. A few other people noticed this and managed to get him outside for some fresh air. As we were walking along the block, someone was trying to get him to laugh and lighten up but it was not working. He was raging about issues with his father. His anger generally had to do with his dad, who was an alcoholic and drug addict who had been in and out of jail most of his life. He was also angry that his mother died when he was a very young child, and according to him, he suffered a lot of abuse at the hands of the foster homes he was placed in until his father was released from jail.

I saw a police car driving past us. I wanted to run towards it and beg for help. I did not, though. Within minutes, the police came by again and I purposely slowed down my walking pace, went behind my husband, and quietly flagged down the officer. I felt ashamed, as I knew this might mean big trouble for him but I was scared my husband would get behind the wheel of the car and drive. I knew he was in no condition to drive since he was having a hard enough time walking! I also knew there would be no way he would allow me to drive, and if he did I was sure I would do something wrong and make him mad. I did not want to risk that either. Fear filled my entire body.

According to him, I drove to slow, too fast, did not get over quick enough, or let too many people cut in front of me. One time he even got angry with me because I put the visor down as the sun was shining in my eyes. He always wanted to drive even when we were dating, and the times he did not have a car, he drove my car. I already had low self-esteem and low self-confidence when we met, it did not take long for his comments and opinions to affect even more how I felt about myself.

As we continued to walk around the block trying to sober up my drunken husband, the officer pulled over and asked if everything was ok. It was obvious it was not. My husband got very belligerent and angry. After a few minutes, the officer gave him the choice to sober up or go to jail. He continued with his angry outburst, this time directed at the officer. He was arrested and put in jail. The officer gave me the information I needed to pick him up in a few hours. We were an hour away from home and I was afraid to go to the county jail alone. I called my mom and stepdad and they came to get me.

When they arrived, it was decided my mom and I would drive back to their place and my stepdad would go to the jail. After a few hours, he arrived with my husband at my mom's. When my husband walked in, he looked very humbled and tired. We got in the car and my stepdad followed us to our apartment, to make sure he was ok to drive. As soon as we got in the car, I knew there would be huge trouble when we got home. My stomach began to turn as I realized he was still very angry. I was trying to talk calmly to him, reassuring him that I called my parents as soon as I could, and telling him "it's ok, you are home now." He was furious at the officer who arrested him. I felt a small sense of relief, as he had no idea that I was the one who flagged the officer down. As we got closer to home, he seemed to get madder and madder. I was getting more and more anxious. I quickly planned that once we arrived and my stepdad said good-bye, I would say our code word and he would not leave me alone with him. Unfortunately, he did not stop to say goodbye, he just waved and left. He had no idea what was taking place inside the car.

As we entered the apartment, I went to turn the light on and he said "NO! NO LIGHTS!" He then pushed me forcefully down into the big chair we had in the front room. He placed his knees on my arms and began punching my face. I remember with the first hit my head turning viciously to the side and literally seeing stars. I was terrified! I lost count of the hits but there were several. He eventually got up and ran to the bedroom crying and saying, "I hit my wife. I can't believe I just hit my wife!" I went to comfort him and tell him I was ok. He ended up pushing me down on the bed and sitting on my chest and arms, pulling my hair and slapping me. I could hardly breathe! I prayed "God please let me live!" Something deep inside me screamed really loud, "STOP! STOP IT!" This seemed to take him out of his frenzy, at least long enough to get off me. He then sat down on the floor next to the bed and cried. I was crying and terrified that I would not live to see the day light. I ran to the bathroom and saw that my face was completely swollen and bloody.

He came into the bathroom and said, "Look what I have done to you!" I tried to comfort him again telling him I loved him and I would be ok. I began praying in my head, "Lord, please just let him pass out so I can escape, I promise I will follow you if you just let me live." I was racked with guilt that maybe I deserved this since I did flag down the officer. I was not even considering this was his fault – his choice – since he chose to drink, he chose to cause his friends to worry about him with his angry outbursts, and he chose to argue with the officer. His issues were bigger than me and had nothing at all to do with me.

After a short time, he finally passed out. I knew I needed to leave. I was nervous that he would wake up and realize I was trying to leave. If he did, I knew I would be dead. I tried to be so quiet. Thankfully, he did not wake up. Once I was outside, I ran to the neighbor's bedroom and began banging on their window. They opened up the curtain, saw me, and immediately let me in their apartment. Once safe inside I began to sob and shake like never before. I called my mom and stepdad and they came at once to get me. The next morning they took me to a doctor. I was examined and had several x-rays. No broken bones, just lots of bruises, swelling and cuts. I had bruises all over my body. I was also in a lot of pain. My body had never felt like that before. During that time as my mom helped care for my bruises and cuts, she did not say anything to me about leaving him, filing charges, or staying with her. She never suggested I should consider seeking counseling or any other kind of help. I almost felt like it was just par for the course in marriage somehow. Looking back, it was as if she was afraid to tell me what to do. I know she loved and cared about me, but she gave me no guidance whatsoever.

Two days passed before he called me. He sounded devastated, sad, and depressed. He promised he would not drink again and he would go to a men's counselor. He vowed to do whatever he needed to do to get me home again. He wanted me back. He loved me. As with the last big incident, he never apologized. He never took responsibility. He insisted it was the officer's fault, which in turn made me feel guilty.

I felt confused. I looked in the mirror at my swollen and bruised face. I was now very aware of what he could do to me but I also felt responsible for him. I never considered living on my own. I was too afraid and felt incapable of doing so. I knew I did not want to live with my mom and stepdad, and the apartment they now had was smaller and there was no room for me. I also knew I did not want to go back to my dad's house. By this time, he was speaking to me but he and my stepmom were going through a divorce and his drinking was getting worse. I wanted so badly to believe my husband was sorry and would change. I did not give him an immediate answer. Within a few hours, he called to tell me again how broken and depressed he was. He said he was scared without me. He told me that he went through all the medicine we had including Tylenol and threw it all away, because he could not trust himself not to do something drastic if I decided not to come back. I felt responsible for his safety and that I needed to go back. If he overdosed, I would have to live with that guilty feeling everyday – like it was my fault because I did not go back to him.

Had he chosen to overdose, I never considered that it would have been HIS choice, not mine. I left him because of *his* actions. I feared for my safety. If he decided to overdose that would have been his choice once again, but instead of facing his own issues he made it my issue. By that time in my life, I was so focused on making decisions and choices that could be expected to make someone else happy, that I just continued doing what I had always done. I continued to feel responsible for his choices and his issues, even though they had NOTHING at all to do with me.

I did go back hoping and praying things would get better. For my own curiosity, I checked all the medications and they were all exactly where they had been all along. Although I had caught him in an obvious lie, I knew I could not point that out; my bruises had not yet healed. I continued with my feelings of loving him and fearing him.

He did go to a men's counselor, and for a while, he worked on his anger issues as well as issues he had with his own father. These counseling appointments did not last very long. He began to feel like he could control his emotions. In my heart, I struggled with my own emotions for him: it was as if he had a love-hate relationship towards me. There were times that he seemed to love me and he was kind and tender towards me. He would shower me with gifts on my birthday or Christmas. Other times it seemed he hated me. Nothing I did was right or pleasing to him, from the clothes I wore, to the way I cleaned things, my weight, and even how I ate my food. These times made it easy for all of my childhood struggles to resurface and push me even further down.

What I Know Now:

1. Once again, I am not responsible for other people's choices or behaviors.
2. There are many red flags or warning signs of abusive relationships. Here are eight that are important not to ignore:
   - One person pushes for a quick and exclusive relationship
   - Is jealous/possessive
   - Blames others for problems or mistakes
   - Makes others feel responsible for their feelings or choices
   - Has unrealistic expectations
   - Angers easily... leaving you feeling like you are walking on egg shells
   - Has a history of abusing others or animals
   - Uses words, facial expressions, or physical violence to intimidate you
3. It is important to recognize that without intensive therapy to get to the root of the problem the abuser will continue to abuse... There is NEVER a reason for abusing someone or accepting abusive behavior.
4. If you or someone you know is in an abusive relationship it is important to seek help immediately. There are many resources available or you can call the National Domestic Violence Hotline at 1-800-799-7233 or www.ndvh.org
5. At that time in my life, I did not recognize that I was in an abusive relationship.
6. People who are diagnosed with Post Traumatic Stress Disorder react to stressful situations by fight, flight, or freeze modes.

7. The layers of guilt and shame I already had were contributing to my PTSD, which made it easier for me to go back into the relationship. I unintentionally took responsibility for his behavior and choices.

8. Psalm 33:20 says, "Our soul waits for the Lord; He is our help and our shield."

Puzzle Piece 8

Secrets

Psalm 130:1-4

Out of the depths I cry to you, O LORD; O Lord, hear my voice. Let your ears be attentive to my cry for mercy. If you, O LORD, kept a record of sins, O Lord, who could stand? But with you there is forgiveness; therefore you are feared.

Shortly after the beating, I learned that I was pregnant for the second time. I had a big secret. My husband did not know that I stopped taking my birth control pills. I wanted a baby. I knew a baby would soften my husband. I knew having a baby would make us a happy family. It would complete us. I was so excited to tell him the news. I assumed he would be just as happy as I was. I was very wrong. He was mad I was pregnant. He told me he was not ready to be a father. He made it clear he did not want to take care of a child at that time in his life. I cried and even begged him to please reconsider. No amount of convincing would work. When I told my mom and stepdad, they agreed with him. They took me for my second abortion. I was devastated and heartbroken. Not only was I losing what I wanted, but also I was aborting my second child. As my mom and stepdad drove me to the appointment, I sat crying in the back seat of the car the whole way to the doctor's office. I was also very mad: I was mad at my husband and I was mad at my mom and stepdad for agreeing with him! I wanted the baby! I planned for the baby and then I had to make everyone else happy once again. My husband never knew about the first abortion, and no one else knew that I purposely tried to become pregnant the second time. Once again, I made the wrong decision. Once again, I was left feeling guilty and ashamed.

I was eighteen years old when I had my second abortion. Even though I was working full time as a receptionist, I was not secure enough financially or emotionally to consider life on my own and certainly not as a single mother. Outside of praying and begging forgiveness once again from God, I kept my secret, my shame, and my pain private. My husband and I never talked about the pregnancy or the abortion again. I continued to feel the heaviness of the scarlet cord around my neck.

Life moved along slowly and insignificantly for a while. While there was never another beating like the first one, there was, however, always the fear. He still erupted into anger, sometimes at me and sometimes about something unrelated to me, but I always feared the consequences of his wrath. He did subtle things like grab my wrists and hold them firmly. He pushed me up against walls and poked me. He yelled and cussed at me. If it seemed to him I had a "look" on my face that he did not like, I was told very harshly to "wipe that look off your face!" It seemed as if the only emotions he could handle from me were love and devotion. It was as if he wanted a robot with no real emotions or feelings, and I was quickly turning into one.

What I Know Now:

1. Secrets are not usually good. If you feel you have to deliberately go behind someone's back to get what you want, pray through your motives and talk to someone who can help you work through the issues.

2. A baby will not "make you a family." There are many wonderful reasons to have a baby but if you think a baby will improve your relationship or somehow make your marriage something it isn't, or change your spouse into someone they are not, those are the wrong reasons to intentionally get pregnant. In an ideal situation I urge you to prayerfully consider talking things over with your spouse and possibly setting up a counseling appointment before you try to manipulate the situation on your own.

3. I have forgiven myself as well as everyone involved. I have also accepted forgiveness from God. Those things did not happen overnight. Forgiveness was a process for me. I still wish I had a forgiveness eraser, but I don't. I will always remember and I will always have regret. My heart is to share with as many women as possible that there are other options besides abortion. If you are in a situation with an unplanned pregnancy I urge you to look through your local resources and talk to a trusted friend or family member.

4. If you have had an abortion please know there is also forgiveness waiting for you. Ephesians 1:7 says, "In Him we have redemption through His blood, the forgiveness of our trespasses, according to the riches of His grace."

Puzzle Piece 9

The Accusation

Psalm 9:9-10

*The LORD also will be a stronghold for the oppressed,
A stronghold in times of trouble; And those who know
Your name will put their trust in You, For You, O
LORD, have not forsaken those who seek You.*

Things began to change one day when my husband met a
guy named Mark. Mark and my husband played on the same
softball team. They quickly became friends. This connection
led to a life-long friendship between Mark's wife Lisa and me.
The couple was newly married, as we were, but the difference
was, they were Christians. They invited us to church. I was so
happy that God placed a Christian couple in our life. I had
been praying that God would open a door for us to go to
church. I had kept my relationship with God private. My
husband and I never discussed religion or anything spiritual. I
now had an opportunity to tell him what I believed in and that
I had accepted Christ a few years earlier while in high school.
After a few short weeks of attending church at The Home
Church in Campbell, California, my husband accepted Christ.

When he raised his hand for the call to accept Christ, we all cried. Mark even gave him his Bible. For a while he really was on fire for Christ. We went to church regularly. He seemed so humbled by recognizing the reality of what Christ had done for him. It was not long before we joined the church. Shortly after we joined the church he became a deacon. Our life was changing for the better. The drinking episodes were almost non-existent. Although his temper seemed to be calmed, I always remained on guard. I continued to love him and fear him at the same time. I never wanted to make him mad and always felt that I had to walk on eggshells. Despite how knotted my stomach was on the inside, outwardly I kept smiling, loving, and hoping.

Right before I found out I was pregnant with my daughter Lauren (we were trying this time) my whole world was rocked. On occasion, we would drive to see my dad and my three youngest siblings, who lived an hour away from us. My dad had started speaking to me again and had even accepted my marriage. He was going through an emotionally hard time as his mother had recently passed away and he was in the midst of divorcing my stepmom. He was also struggling to raise my three younger siblings as a single father. We would take turns having the kids spend weekends with us. My younger sister Shelli spent a lot more time with us than anyone of the others did. She and I were very close. We were planning to go camping with her in the coming weekend when my dad called to tell me he had something very important to talk to me about. He wanted to meet with me, and told me not to tell my husband. I did not know what to expect. I had no idea if this was good news or bad. I met my dad and sister at our apartment.

Once they arrived at our apartment, we all sat down on the couch and my dad got up and began to pace the front room floor. I could tell he and my sister had been crying and this was going to be really bad news. I was not prepared for what my dad was about to tell me. My dad told me that my husband had been molesting my sister! I felt light headed and my heart was pounding and aching all at the same time. After a brief conversation, my dad was insistent that I leave with them to go back to his house. I was scared and very confused. I grabbed my purse and left with my dad and sister. I was sickened by the things my dad was telling me. I felt guilty that I had not protected my sister. I was in shock. Once we arrived at my dad's house I called my husband and told him what my dad had said. My husband was adamant that he was innocent. He was very calm and reassuring. I was completely confused. I truly did not know what to believe. I did not think my sister would lie or make this up but at the same time, my husband was strongly denying the claim.

My husband and my sister were both adamant about their claims. I remained in turmoil. I did not know whom to believe. I felt trapped. I felt no matter what I decided I was losing something. Nothing would ever be the same again. After much heartache, I made the decision to go home to my husband. He wanted me there and at the time, I did not want to believe it could be true. As I made that choice I struggled with guilt and shame. What if he really did do the things my sister said he did? The decision to go home made the weight of my scarlet cord feel heavier than it had felt in a long time.

My dad's response to my decision was to cut off all contact between my siblings and me. He also filed molestation charges against my husband. While I understood why he did so, it was an incredibly painful process. Once the charges were filed against my husband, things seemed to progress quickly. According to my husband, he took a lie detector test and passed. There were also numerous interviews and conversations with the police. I kept looking for evidence that I thought would be irrefutable.

Could he have done it? Was there anything that had happened in the past that was a red flag? There was one incident, but at the time I was too scared to tell anyone about it. As I mentioned earlier, it was not unusual for us kids to share a bed growing up. One night my sister, who was fourteen at the time, was staying the weekend with my husband and me. I had never given a second thought to having one of the younger kids in my bed. It was pure innocence on my part. Something woke me that night and I saw my husband reaching over me towards her. When I opened my eyes and asked, "What are you doing?", he became VERY angry with me and said, "GO BACK TO SLEEP! You don't know what you are talking about you *#*!." This invoked fear in me, as he had not displayed that kind of anger towards me in a while. I was scared of what he might do to me, and I certainly did not want him to harm my sister. I began to question myself, wondering if I saw what I thought I saw. Maybe I was wrong. I wondered why he became so angry. I quickly rolled over towards my sister and closed my eyes. I did not sleep the rest of the night. When morning finally came, no one said a word about it. I foolishly never even questioned my sister about it. That particular incident was **not** listed in the police report, which only made my confusion worse. My husband continued to claim his innocence. My sister continued to accuse him. I wanted to believe both of them. I wanted undeniable proof one way or the other. I was so confused!

As the months passed by, I heard from my stepmom that my dad had made a decision to move. He was by that time divorced from her, and after my grandmother passed away, he and my grandfather wanted to move back "home" to Alabama. At that point the investigation on my husband seemed to stop. I do not know exactly why things were not pursued. Was it because he was found innocent? Was it because there was lack of evidence? Was it because my dad moved to another state? Were the charges dropped? Where was the truth? As hard as it was, I just marched forward in life, pushing even more things under my rug.

It was several months later before I finally had a chance to see my brother and two sisters again. I was very pregnant at the time. My stepmom was getting married and she was determined to bring "peace" between my sister and me. She arranged a meeting where we saw one another without my dad knowing. When we finally saw one another, with tears in our eyes, we uncomfortably hugged. I could see the pain in her eyes. I battled with many emotions... guilt, doubt, anxiousness, anger, and even fear – not at my sister, but at the entire situation. We were not encouraged to talk about the accusation, only to make peace. It appeared we had. It took almost twenty more years before we could talk about all of it again, for me to ask her direct questions and find the answers that I needed, to forgive myself, and to move forward.

What I Know Now:

1. According to Dictionary.com the word molestation means to bother, interfere with, or annoy; to make indecent sexual advances; to assault sexually.

2. My response to the situation with my sister was affected by Post Traumatic Stress Disorder.

3. During most of my marriage I stayed in the freeze or fight mode, although, *my* fight mode was not what most would think of the word "fight." My fight mode was trying to stay one step ahead, protecting myself or those close to me, and at times even protecting my husband. I responded the only way I knew how at the time.

4. If you or someone you know is being sexually abused please tell a trusted adult and contact your local law enforcement.

Puzzle Piece 10

Happiness and Dysfunction

John 14:27

Peace I leave with you; My peace I give to you; not as the world gives do I give to you Do not let your heart be troubled, nor let it be fearful.

October 1988 was one of the most special times of my life! My daughter Lauren was born. Being a mom was a dream come true for me. I instantly fell in love with my sweet baby girl. I had never known the true power of love until the very moment that I held her for the first time and looked into her eyes. Having our daughter also made my husband respond to me in a much kinder and gentler way. The moment she was born and he cut her umbilical cord I saw something different in his eyes. He wanted to be the father he never had to our daughter. I was overjoyed with the birth of my daughter but I also had a deep sadness inside of my heart. I longed for my dad and my family to share in the moment with me.

Right before my dad moved out of state he called me to say that he wanted to see me and meet his granddaughter Lauren. She was almost a year old and he had never seen her nor held her. Lauren was his first grandchild. I could hardly contain myself when I answered the phone and heard my dad's voice say, "Sheryl, this is Dad." I had been praying for that phone call. I missed my dad. I wanted him to be a part of Lauren's life and mine. I wondered if he was going to move to Alabama without saying goodbye and without ever embracing his first grandchild. With his call I was very eager to push everything under the rug deeper than before, just to have my dad back in my life again. I was not sure if my husband would agree to let me go and say goodbye, but he did. He told me I had to do it during the week while he was at work, which meant that I had to take the four-year-old girl I was babysitting at the time with Lauren and me. Maybe he thought I would not want to go if I had to ask her parents since it would require an hour's drive to get there. I was not sure they would give me their permission, but I felt it was worth asking. I explained the situation as best as I could without telling too many details. At the end of our conversation, they gave me their permission. I was relieved and grateful.

I felt many emotions as we made the hour-long drive to see my dad. I was excited to be able to see my family again. I was also nervous my dad might bring the molestation accusation up and try to convince me to move with him to Alabama. I was not ready to make a choice like that. I was also facing the reality and the deep sadness that this might possibly be the last time I saw my dad, grandfather, and siblings, since they were moving so far away. I knew we could not afford airplane tickets, and if we could, I did not think my husband would want me to go. On the other side of my emotions, I was very grateful for another chance with my dad. It had been almost two years since I last saw him and my grandfather. I was more than ready for a chance to reunite with them.

Once we arrived at my grandfather's home, my dad and grandfather came outside to greet us. I quickly unbuckled the car seats and once I had all of us out of the van, my dad walked up to me and we hugged and cried. My dad and grandfather loved Lauren instantly. She was a little shy at first but she quickly warmed up to both of them. I brought my camera and made sure I took photos of Lauren with my dad and grandfather and I have a very special picture that my grandfather took of my dad and me together.

No one ever said a word about my husband or the accusations. I was relieved that my dad never asked me if I wanted to come with him to Alabama. We went about our conversation as if the past two years had never happened. We never said "his name" and managed to talk around anything that had to do with him at all. My dad generously offered to pay airfare for Lauren and me to come and visit him each summer. I was thrilled at the thought of having him and my brother and two sisters back in my life once again. I was hopeful that my husband would agree to these visits if my dad was the one paying.

When it was time to leave, I tried to put on my brave face and not let my tears fall. I made it until I turned the key to start the van. My tears flowed quietly and softy as I sat in the front seat and drove the hour back home. I made myself stop crying as I took the exit off the freeway that led to my home. I did not want anyone to know that I had been crying.

At home things had settled down a lot for us, as not only did we have a baby but we also had custody of my husband's thirteen year-old brother Leo. Leo came to live with us right at the beginning of everything with my sister. I was happy to have him live with us, though I was not thinking what would be best for Leo. I was thinking of the safety of having someone else in our home. In the end, it also turned out to be the best for Leo. He lacked discipline and stability in his life while living with his mother. He and my husband had the same father. Their father continued to battle with drugs and alcohol and was in and out of jail. He was unable to care for

Leo. Under our care, Leo agreed to stay in school and stay out of trouble.

During that time, my husband tried to portray the image of being a "good guy." He wanted people to see him as a provider, a father, a good husband, and even a Christian. He worked at changing his image. We continued to go to church as a family each Sunday. He kept his temper under control. He was positive and encouraging. These changes lasted for a while, but slowly the old behaviors crept back in.

When his old behaviors and patterns started slipping back in, he again acted as if he loved me and hated me all at the same time. He would show me his tender side, shower me with gifts, and tell me how much he loved me and needed me. For a while he even prayed with me. He was always a great charmer. It was not always abusive and he was not always angry. It was confusing to say the least. He would shower me with affection and then completely destroy my self confidence and self esteem with negative comments about me, my body, or how I did or did not do something correctly or to his liking. It made it easier for me to believe his negative comments, more than his positive ones, because of how I felt about myself. Little by little he filled me with self-doubt, creating a greater lack of self-confidence. He would constantly tell me I was "vanilla," boring, predictable, and he was "rocky road," spontaneous and adventurous. I began to believe him. He would say I was nice, and that I would not ever say or think anything mean about anyone, not even an ax murderer. He was very good at controlling me.

He created expectations of me that even after our divorce I would follow. While I do not believe he intentionally set out to treat me the way he did, I did not know any better. Neither did I have the confidence, self esteem, example or experience to realize that was not love, that was **not** how two people should treat each other in *any* kind of a relationship. I was also functioning within the realms of PTSD.

During our marriage, my husband would at times disappear for hours, always coming home with an elaborate story of how he rescued someone from a burning car or helped a stranded motorist. There were never any news reports or acknowledgments for these "acts of heroism," and inwardly I never believed him, but I never questioned him or his stories. There were also plenty of times when there were simply no excuses. When those times happened, I knew not to question him at all.

One December we were going to get a Christmas tree and Lauren and I were waiting for him to get home. He was several hours late. When he finally arrived home I could tell he had been drinking. I showed my displeasure somehow and for the first and only time he used Lauren against me. He took her to get the tree knowing he had been drinking, and knowing I was scared. My punishment, for showing my displeasure, was not being allowed to go with them. I felt it was almost as if he was daring me to stop him. I knew if I tried to take Lauren away from him it could endanger her. I also knew if I tried to argue with him that I would be opening myself up for a consequence. I remember that as soon as the door closed I fell on my knees and prayed as hard as I could for their safe return. God answered that prayer. They did return safe and sound about an hour later. We decorated the tree and never talked about the situation. I made sure never to cross that line again or at least not to allow Lauren to be available for his manipulation. I tried even harder to be one-step ahead of him. I was good at anticipating his next move, all the while loving him, serving him, and telling myself "this is what you get when you don't follow God's plan." The scarlet cord continued to feel heavier around my neck.

As my husband's career began to take off, he started hanging out after work to have drinks with his co-workers. That led to many nights of not hearing from him or seeing him until after two o'clock in the morning. I never confronted him.

I never told anyone. I just acted normal each time he came home. I never knew if he was simply hanging out with the guys, seeing someone else, or if he was dead on the side of the road. I internalized my fears and concerns. I was holding it all in. We were attending church, but I did not confide in anyone who could help. I just kept praying and keeping things to myself.

Each time he came home I was relieved he was alive but I was also very mad that he had stayed out all night drinking. He made sure I would not confront him by doing things to "remind" me of what he was capable of. One night in particular he came home after the bar closed and I was awake. (I was always awake but always pretended to be asleep.) I heard him open his nightstand drawer and take something out. I was filled with fear because that was where I knew he kept his huge knife. That night, I never fell back asleep. When he woke up the next morning, he had his hand under his pillow. I could still smell the alcohol on his breath and his eyes were bloodshot. He looked at me and pulled his hand out from under his pillow still holding the knife. I was so scared! He looked at me and asked, "DID YOU PUT THIS HERE?" I answered as calmly as I could, "No." I was afraid to tell him that he took the knife from the drawer and placed it under his pillow the night before, because I did my best to feign being asleep when he came home, and I did not want him to know I had been awake. I felt that would somehow make him mad, plus the fact that he put the knife close to my face and told me "This is dangerous! I could have killed you last night, I didn't put this here!" I was scared to death. I did not know if he was going to push the blade into my face or stab me in the chest. I answered as calmly as I could again, "No, I did not put the knife there." He looked at me, sat up, and then put the knife back in the nightstand drawer. He got out of bed and went to bathroom and took a shower. I was so panicked and relieved at the same time that my stomach was very nauseous. I was sweating, and my heart was racing. I needed to keep busy so I made the bed and then I played with Lauren, doing whatever I could to stay busy and out of his way. Once out of the shower he dressed, ate breakfast, and we went about our day... back to "normal."

<u>What I Know Now:</u>

1. While I was grateful to reconcile with my dad and family it was unfortunate that the situation with my sister was swept under the rug never to be brought up again by my dad or me.

2. The relationship I had in my marriage was not a healthy loving relationship.

3. The intimidation that my husband displayed towards me had to do with him and his issues, and had nothing to do with me. It is never appropriate to intimidate or bully anyone.

4. I can now see how, as one of my doctors said, that I was primed for an abusive relationship. My scarlet cord had already been formed and I was already struggling with self worth, self-esteem, self-doubt, guilt, shame, and fear. The issues and struggles my husband had, as well as my feelings about myself, set the stage for our dysfunctional abusive relationship.

5. I was already having panic and anxiety attacks during this time, and I didn't realize it. Emotionally I was fighting for my life.

Puzzle Piece 11

The Affair

Psalm 147:3
He heals the brokenhearted And binds up their wounds.

My husband suddenly began to act more jealous and started to accuse me of things like looking at men or thinking thoughts about other men. He would come home at odd times throughout the day, to get a soda or use the bathroom. While he always said he was out running work errands or on his lunch break, it appeared to me that he was checking up on me. I did home day care during that time, so I was always home and always had children with me. I soon became suspicious of his behaviors and found motel receipts and photos of another woman. It was someone he worked with. I was devastated. I was mad. I also knew I did not have the courage to confront him face to face. I finally confided in my friend Lisa. By that time, we had been friends for a few years and she saw through some of the things that were quietly going on, although that was the first time I confided in her. Together we created a plan for Lauren and me to leave. I included my mom, stepdad, and even Leo, his brother who was still living with us.

After he left for work one day, Lisa came to get Lauren and me. She was going to take us to her parents' house in Hollister, California, about an hour away. Oddly enough, I remember realizing I had not ironed his shirts for the week, and as Lisa was helping me get our suitcases in the car I said, "I need to iron his shirts before I leave." She looked at me and very firmly said, "No! Sheryl you are not going to iron his shirts! He can iron his own shirts." I knew he would need his shirts ironed for the week and it would make him mad that they were not ready but I left them there all wrinkled and crumpled on top of the dryer.

I struggled with leaving Leo there but it did not seem right to take him with me, and he wanted to stay. At that point in his life he had a job, a steady girlfriend, and was finishing high school. I felt he could take care of himself, and he did.

My husband's affair devastated me, but deep down I was hopeful that it would finally lead to my freedom. I knew that I could not ask for a divorce. I was afraid of what he might do to me if he thought the divorce was my idea. He needed to ask for it. If our marriage was ending it would have to be HIS decision.

In the end, he confessed the affair and asked for forgiveness. Again he told me how he needed me and loved me. I felt trapped. I felt I had no choice but to forgive and go home, so I packed our bags and we went home. But something had changed deep in my heart towards him during that time. My feelings for him never returned, but his infidelity did.

What I Know Now

1. The affair was not my fault. I am not responsible for other people's choices.

2. I did not have the courage or ability to confront my husband face to face. I felt he would deny it or somehow I would be to blame. I was afraid of his reaction. I felt the only way I could let him know I knew was by secretly leaving.

3. The affair shocked me but at the same time it also helped me stop protecting my husband and face the reality of who he was and the type of marriage we had.

4. I was beginning to have courage and see the truth, but I was also still very fearful of him.

5. I was afraid that he would take my daughter away from me. I felt as if the best way to protect her was to go back and try to make it work.

6. Many of my fears stemmed from the stories and experiences I had from my parents divorce.

7. I was still responding in the fight, flight, or freeze mode of PTSD.

Puzzle Piece 12

My Mom

Deuteronomy 31:6
Be strong and courageous, do not be afraid, or
tremble at them, for the LORD your God is the one
who goes with you He will not fail you or forsake
you.

Sprinkled in throughout my marriage were moments of what I call "alcoholic outbursts" from my mom. I had discovered shortly after moving in with my mom and stepdad, when I was a teenager, that my mom at times would drink, get drunk, become angry, and then all of the sudden the alcohol would disappear from our home and life just continued on. She was never violent during these times, though she would become argumentative and angry. Things usually stayed within the confines of my stepdad and mom's private relationship.

After I was married, my mom developed a habit of getting drunk and then calling my husband and me to come and rescue her. We would go and pick her up from her home until she sobered up and wanted to go back. We would sit and listen to her go on and on about my stepdad, never saying anything specific or incriminating. In an odd way, my husband seemed to enjoy this "dance" with my mom. It was a like a game to him to try to decipher what it was that she was hiding or trying to say. Neither of us could ever figure it out. I dreaded those phone calls. These episodes were not daily, weekly or even monthly. At times my mom could go a whole year without touching any alcohol. Then something or someone would trigger her and she would start with one or two drinks, and progress each day until there was some sort of outburst.

My mom and stepdad were both very good at keeping things between themselves, but that seemed to change as I got older. I began to see more and more. The episodes were almost always the same. She would be very drunk. She would become very angry and accusatory. If my stepdad could not keep my mom's drinking confined to their house and others were involved (a phone call), there would be a big apology afterwards and a promise not to have any more alcohol in the house. I was relieved when that part happened because I knew it would be true, at least for a while. Once again, after each outburst, we never talked about it. After the apology nothing was ever explained, and professional help was never sought. That was the vicious cycle for years.

Usually when my mom was drunk and complaining about my stepdad, she would say that he was mean and controlling. She would say, "Sheryl you just don't know all the things he has done and is doing to me." She was always very secretive and would never be specific. I had a hard time believing there was any truth to those claims, especially since she always wanted to go home once she sobered up, and after the apology the two of them continued to go about life as usual. I do not think my mom was intentionally lying. I think somewhere deep inside her she believed the things she said and alluded to. When my mom was sober she said my stepdad was her best friend. He was always the protector and provider. I never heard him raise his voice to my mom. I never saw or heard him do anything remotely inappropriate. With my own experiences, I do know, as an adult, that things can still go on behind closed doors that children and even grown children may never know about. That thought made me feel I had to be "on guard" at all times.

One drunken outburst caused me to question my mother's mental stability. That time she said that my stepdad was going to kill all of us. Some of the things she told me really scared me. While I did not believe my stepdad would actually do those things, my mom was convincing enough that we "escaped" to a local motel. When I refused to buy her more alcohol at the motel, she was suddenly no longer afraid to go home. She confessed that my stepdad did *not* have a plan to kill us after all. We ended up in a very intense argument. The result was that she took a cab back home because I refused to take her. She called me the next day to say she was sorry and there would be no more alcohol in the house once again. I remember feeling a wide range of emotions and feeling very unsure of who my mom really was and who my stepdad really was.

As we always did, we just went back to "normal" and never talked about the situation again. With years of training, we were all very good at putting things under the rug and never dealing with them again.

What I Know Now:

1. My mom had a very traumatic childhood. Her mother was an alcoholic and her stepfather was in the army and rarely home. She has never known her biological father. I know she was neglected and emotionally (and maybe physically) abused as a child. She was one of six children in a very dysfunctional family.

2. I love my mom and pray for her constantly, but I still have many unanswered questions regarding our past, and who she is today.

3. Alcoholics are unstable; therefore, trying to have a relationship with anyone who struggles with alcoholism is challenging.

4. Binge drinking is a form of alcoholism.

5. Alcoholism can be treated but it is a choice.

6. My mom's past, problems, and issues are bigger than I am and I cannot help her. I love her and I encourage her, but the rest is up to her. She needs professional help.

7. I know my mom loves me.

Puzzle Piece 13

Divorce

Isaiah 41:13
For I am the LORD your God, who upholds your right hand, Who says to you, "Do not fear, I will help you."

As I struggled to balance my relationship with my mom and my marriage, I did my best to keep my head up and just keep moving forward. I continued to hide things under the rug and I continued to feel the weight of the scarlet cord around my neck. By that time in my life, my husband and I no longer attended church regularly. I continued to pray on my own, although my relationship with Christ was then based more on fear and seeking protection, than in the relationship God truly desires from me.

Eighteen months after my husband confessed his first affair and told me that he wanted our marriage to work, his second affair ended our marriage of almost nine years. Strangely enough, my daughter Lauren was the same age I was when my parents divorced, almost five.

Lauren and I went to Alabama that summer, as we usually did, for a week at my dad's expense. My husband always encouraged us to go. Looking back, I think he enjoyed the week alone. We never really talked about what he did while I was gone, and he never really asked me much about my visit. When we returned home from that particular visit, however, things seemed very different. I could not pinpoint what it was, but I felt something. I honestly had been noticing things for a few months prior to my visit with my dad, but had resigned myself to thinking that was just the way things were. The day after we arrived home at the end of our summer visit with my dad, my husband sat me down in the front room and told me how he didn't want our marriage to end with him cheating, and he didn't want things to end on a bad note because of him. He was tired of living a life he was not happy with. He wanted a divorce, but he wanted us to remain friends.

I remember feeling scared, mad, sad, and relieved, all at the same time. My mind and heart were racing. I thought it was odd that he did not want our marriage to end because of "him" or his actions. Was he oblivious to all he had been doing to me since we started dating? I also thought it was interesting that he had also been unhappy all that time. I came to find out that there was another (much younger) woman he had met at work. According to him they had not yet become intimate, but it was obvious he was ready to cross that line. He may not have had sex with her yet, but he was already having an emotional affair with her and had been counting down the days until he would tell me.

Suddenly I felt a small backbone growing inside of me. I firmly told him, "If you take me down this path there is no turning back." I wanted to make it clear there would be no turning back since a divorce was HIS choice now. He agreed. I was determined to stay strong on this. I knew if I allowed him to continue to move in and out of my life that I would never be able to move forward. I was now ready to face life on my own with Lauren. He wanted us to share legal custody of Lauren, but willingly gave me physical custody of her. He said he would always provide for us. Lauren and I stayed in the house we were renting and he moved to a nearby apartment.

Every marriage should be based on trust, honesty, and open communication. We had none of that. I soon found out he had racked up close to $30,000 in credit card debt. Several of the cards were in my name and I never knew they existed. To my surprise, he took financial responsibility for all but one card that only had a few thousand dollars on it.

During that time, I continued to face all the emotions from one extreme to another, sometimes all at once. There were moments when I did feel stronger. There were also moments of extreme grief and sorrow. No matter how much I wanted to be away from him or how much I feared him, life with him was the only life I knew. I was also giving up - again - on my dream of a family.

When I told my dad I was getting a divorce he was happy and said, "It's about time!" That was all. We still never talked about "him," my sister's accusation, or anything related to my soon-to-be ex-husband. My mom and stepdad wanted to be supportive of me and help me out as much as they could. Although I did not confide in them all that was going on, I thought it was odd that they waited until I told them I was getting a divorce to tell me they had never liked or trusted him. My mom and stepdad said that after the first beating they would look for new bruises on my body, but they never asked me about it. We never talked about what happened that night. They never asked if the abuse continued. I wondered if they would they have said or done anything had they suspected abuse? Was I such a good actor that I put on the perfect front, or were they just accustomed to looking the other way?

What I Know Now:

1. All of the emotions I battled were normal. Divorce is difficult no matter the condition of your marriage.

2. Once my husband opened the door for divorce I responded with the flight mode of PTSD. This gave me the courage I needed to move forward and not to allow him back into my life physically and emotionally.

3. Even though I was ready to move forward in my life, I felt that being divorced added to the weight of my scarlet cord, my shame. I struggled with knowing that God hates divorce.

4. The Bible is clear that God hates divorce: Malachi 2:16a "For 'I hate divorce,' says the Lord the God of Israel." It is also clear that the reason He hates divorce is because it breaks the covenant (promise) made at the time of a marriage between two people. While divorce is a biblically allowed option, the challenge for two committed Christians headed toward divorce is to seek out all Godly help, support and prayers – at ALL costs.

5. The Bible is also clear there is forgiveness: Acts 13:38-39 "Therefore let it be known to you, brethren, that through Him forgiveness of sins is proclaimed to you, and through Him everyone who believes is freed from all things, from which you could not be freed through the Law of Moses."

Puzzle Piece 14

A Single Mom

Psalm 34:18-19

The LORD is near to the brokenhearted. And saves those who are crushed in spirit. Many are the afflictions of the righteous, But the LORD delivers him out of them all.

Now that I was on my own, I knew I could not rest – I had to be strong for my daughter's sake. As I battled all the mixed emotions inside of me I was also dealing with Lauren's devastation as a result of her dad leaving the family. I was also feeling guilty for hurting my daughter in the way that *I* was hurt when *my* parents divorced. I never wanted to put her in my shoes. Even though it was my choice to get married, I was mad at God. Didn't I put up with enough from my husband for God to bless the marriage anyway? I felt like I willingly sacrificed too much for my dream. Once in the marriage, I followed all the rules. I did everything I could to please him. I thought if I kept the house clean, ironed the shirts, made dinner on time, did all the things he wanted and expected, as well as took all he dished out to me, then he would love me and our marriage would be complete. That is not what happened.

I had no idea that was not God's ideal design for marriage. The way I felt about my husband is not how God intended women to feel towards their spouse. The way he treated me is not the way God intended husbands to treat their wives.

As I struggled through my emotions I wanted to do whatever I could to make the change as easy as possible for Lauren. I knew I would have to continue to "play nice" with her dad. I knew I needed to include him in things with Lauren. I also knew I should never confront him on things that might trigger an angry response. However, if he ever physically touched me in an abusive way, I had decided that I would fight back, and I would fight hard. I have never had to test my decision, as he has never physically abused or touched me again. In spite of that, I still feared him. I knew what he was capable of doing.

Now that my daughter was a child of divorce I wanted to spare her some of the things I experienced as a child. I was very careful about how I spoke of her dad. I did not want her to feel the things that I felt as a child. I felt confident that he would never do anything inappropriate to her. That feeling may seem irrational, but God gave me peace about it. I also did my best to insure she knew right from wrong early on in her life, including the difference between good touches and bad touches even from Mommy and Daddy. I made a point of making her independent at an early age: getting dressed on her own, going to the bathroom, and bathing on her own. I was not worried that he would beat her because he was very careful not to display any of those behaviors in front of her or anyone else.

Women in abusive relationships function differently than women in loving, trusting marriages. I was always on guard, always prepared. If you were to read my journals that I kept from the very beginning of my pregnancy with Lauren until the separation, you would have thought things were good. It's not that I was lying, I was just being very careful. He could read my journal at anytime. I knew I needed to watch myself in person and on paper.

I was very overwhelmed with being on my own. I had never been alone before. From birth someone was always taking care of me, my dad, my mom, my husband. In my marriage I had never been allowed to open any bills or look over our checkbook. I could open letters addressed to me but never any bills. I knew nothing about budgeting, credit cards, finance charges, or paying bills. On top of trying to learn about all that, I was very lonely, especially when Lauren was overnight at her dad's.

I began to rebel and ease back into old habits of seeking out unhealthy relationships. Those relationships had no depth, no love, and no security attached with them. Although I made a point to stay away from men I saw as intimidating or aggressive, during this time in my life I still ended up making some very bad decisions. It was a season in my life full of regrets and memories that I wish I could erase. Once again in my life I was "wasting too many kisses" on undeserving men. Was I as alone as I thought I was? No. Even during this time, God still had His hand on me waiting patiently for me to turn to Him, wanting a real relationship with me. It was hard for me to consider this thought back then, but it is true.

I continued to struggle emotionally and spiritually. I found myself wondering why I married the man I did and why I stayed so long. I had many questions. I knew I needed help in making sense of all the puzzle pieces. I decided I needed to open up to someone who could help me sort through my mess. I went back to the church my husband and I first attended when he accepted Christ. I set up a counseling appointment. I only went two times. The woman counselor listened and prayed with me and at the end of our hour together she told me to keep praying. I do not think she really believed any of the things I told her, nor did I feel she had any understanding of the struggles I was feeling. I felt alone and ashamed. I felt the weight of my scarlet cord around my neck. I decided it was probably best to continue to carry it all inside. That was what I was used to doing. I hoped that maybe if I was good enough, at some point God would forgive me. I wish I had known this scripture then – Ephesians 2:8:

"For by grace you have been saved through faith; and that not of yourselves, it is the gift of God."

What I Know Now:

1. I felt like a failure. I tried with all of my heart to love and serve my husband. I felt nothing would ever be enough for him. I also felt that I let our daughter down. I did not want her to deal with the same issues that I did as a child of divorced parents. The patterns of shame and guilt continued to follow me.

2. I recognize now that I was not a failure. I did not fail my marriage or my daughter.

3. I needed professional counseling. The counseling I received at the time was from a church trained volunteer. While I feel this type of counseling can serve a purpose in church, it was not what I needed then. I needed a professional to help me identify areas in my life and help me walk through the process of the divorce.

4. I was still looking for someone to fill my emotional needs.

5. Because I was still filled with guilt and shame, I continued to settle for less than God's best for me.

Puzzle Piece 15

Meeting Jungle Doug

James 1:22

But prove yourselves doers of the word, and not merely hearers who delude themselves.

After struggling through almost two years as a divorced woman and a single mom, I started figuring out things in life that I enjoyed. I tried to do things, try things, and even eat things that *I* wanted, not what I thought someone wanted for me. I was experimenting with my freedom.

I had started listening to a local country radio station every day. I loved the morning show with Gary Scott Thomas and Jungle Doug! I loved Doug's voice from the very beginning. He seemed like a genuinely nice guy on the radio. He was also funny and he made me laugh. Although I had a boyfriend at the time, I still wanted to meet him.

I heard them say on the radio that Doug was going to be at a local business for a radio remote. I was excited that I would finally have a chance to meet "Jungle Doug." I wanted to see the face behind the voice I heard each morning. After I met him we quickly became friends. While I was only dating one person, Jungle Doug was involved with many women. As we started talking, we realized we had some similarities. He was previously married, a Christian, but right then he was drinking in what the world had to offer, and so was I.

It did not take long before things heated up in our friendship. I had realized for a while that the relationship I was in was not going to be a long-term relationship with any depth. I ended that relationship and allowed things with Jungle Doug to progress to a dating relationship, and then into an exclusive dating relationship. Something that attracted us to one another besides physical attributes was the fact that we were both Christians, even though we were not living as Christians. We both said we wanted God in our lives – later.

I was falling hard for him. Not only did I feel attracted to him physically, but emotionally as well. I felt safe around him. I called him my "KISA" – Knight in Shining Armor. He also really cared for and liked my daughter. He never minded including her in things. He enjoyed playing games, reading books, and even played Barbie's with her. I knew the next person I would marry would have to accept Lauren and me as a total package. No ifs, ands, or buts. He did. Lauren also liked and accepted her "Jungle."

We both entered our relationship with lots of emotional and spiritual baggage. We became engaged and he moved in with Lauren and me, into our two-bedroom apartment in Sunnyvale, California. Things went well for a while. We said that once we got married THEN we would go to church. Deep down we knew that sex before marriage was not how God intended sex to be between a man and a woman. God created sex for pleasure, and procreation, but at the same time, pleasure in the confines of marriage, in a safe, loving, monogamous, and committed relationship. At the time, we lived as if God had blinders on and could not see the choices we were making.

I remember my dear friend Lisa when she confronted me about our living together. She was supposed to be in our wedding. She called and said, "Sheryl, I love you and I think Doug is a great guy. I think you both love the Lord, but what you are doing is wrong and I cannot support you like this. I cannot be in your wedding. I will be there for you but I cannot stand up with you." I knew she was right, but I did not want to risk losing the one good man I ever had in my life. She followed that quick conversation up with a letter. I still have that letter today. I use it as part of my testimony.

In the letter, Lisa told me how she loved Lauren and me and how God could never bless a relationship in sin. She lovingly but firmly challenged me to do the right thing. I told Doug about the letter. We both knew she was right but we were not worried about God at that time. In our minds, God would come later.

Months went by and I began to notice changes in Doug. He seemed suddenly distant, unsure. As the date for my bridal shower neared he told me he was not sure about getting married at that time. After lots of heartache on my part we made the decision to cancel the bridal shower. Unlike the patterns I had always been in, I tried to talk to him. I did not want to push things under the rug, but he would not tell me anything. I was wondering if that was the part when God would not bless our relationship. I decided I needed to go back to church. I needed to seek God. Once again, I was seeking God for protection – not for my physical safety this time – but for my heart. I still did not get it that God wants a relationship with me and I could come to Him for more than just protection.

I called Doug's best friend Hans, who I knew was a grounded and respectful Christian, and asked him to tell me about his church. I knew it was local and Lisa had said it was a good church. I remember we went several times together. Doug would not come with us. Lisa had begun to encourage me to get into counseling. She recommended a great Christian counselor (Dr. Don Phillips) who she and her husband had used when they were struggling through some marital issues. I asked Doug to come with me. He agreed. I was beginning to see that my relationship with God needed some major attention, as well as learning new truths about God – who *He* is and who *I* am in Christ – truths I had not heard or realized before. I was also recognizing my relationships with men were usually unhealthy. Even though I made sure to stay away from abusive men, I was still putting too much trust and hope in one man. That trust and hope is reserved for God. I began to learn about healthy boundaries and how to let God be the main man in my life. I did not need a man to fill that void, because God was willing and able.

As we continued with a few counseling appointments Doug still seemed unsure. I began to question what it was that I had done wrong to make him suddenly question "us." Why was he suddenly changing his mind about me? What did I do wrong? Was he lying to me with all the cards, notes, and words of affirmation the whole time? Had I fallen for a man and been duped? I thought we were on the same page. I allowed myself to "cross the line" with him emotionally, something I had NEVER done before with any man, not even my first husband. My guard was totally down. I was so scared. I felt very vulnerable. I was also very mad at myself for allowing it to happen to me. As the wedding date was fast approaching we decided to do the unthinkable (at least in my mind) and postpone the wedding. He made all the calls. He even stayed at a hotel a few nights. While I felt I had done something wrong in every previous relationship, I couldn't figure out how I could have messed this one up. My scarlet cord was still hanging tightly around my neck.

What I Know Now:

1. Doug and I were putting ourselves and our desires ahead of God.

2. As my pastor, Chris Williamson, once said, "If you want to be covered by the will of God you must choose to come under the covering and stay there."

3. I allowed myself to fall back into old patterns and tried to take responsibility for someone else's feelings or problems as I began to question what had I done to change his feelings about me.

Puzzle Piece 16

Truth

Ezekiel 18:31-32

Cast away from you all your transgressions, which you have committed and make yourselves a new heart and a new spirit! For why will you die, O house of Israel? "For I have no pleasure in the death of anyone who dies," declares the Lord GOD. "Therefore, repent and live."

After months of confusion and the on-again off-again feeling I was getting from Doug, everything came to a head one night in May of 1996. That night, Doug gave me a letter that explained it all. I only read the first few lines of the letter before I saw all I needed to see. He admitted to seeing someone else. I was completely devastated. I was broken. I literally felt myself snap inside. I ripped the letter to shreds and threw it at him. I vaguely remember calling my mom telling her to come and get Lauren. I had enough sense in me to know I did not want her to hear or see whatever might happen next. I took my engagement ring off and threw it as hard as I could at his face. I remember running around the apartment and taking all the pictures of us I could find and ripping them to shreds, all the while crying and yelling at him. I pulled his clothes from the closet and threw them on the floor. I called his mom and told her what he had been doing. He kept trying to calm me down and talk to me. I wanted him to know how much he hurt me. I wanted him to feel my pain. I had let my guard down and I trusted him with all my heart.

The way I was expressing myself was new to me. I was not use to showing my emotions like that. I allowed myself to feel something AND show it on the outside. It went on for what seemed like hours. I do not know how or when but at some point I became exhausted, laid down on the bed, and fell asleep. Doug stayed by my side throughout the entire time. I do not remember the exact details, I just remember waking up and seeing him looking at me and him saying, "I am so sorry. I love you." I wanted so badly to believe him but with the history I have in relationships "sorry" did not mean much. I do not know why but I remember saying I loved him, too. I remember feeling confused because I *did* love him, but at that moment, I also hated him. I knew I was not ready to forgive him but somehow saying "I love you," back opened the door for forgiveness and freedom - Freedom for both of us.

I thought it might be helpful to have Doug tell his story.

I was born to a single mom until I was 11 and she married my stepdad. I have never met my biological father. I spent my senior high school year in Germany, as an exchange student.

Germany was a great experience for me. I grew a lot from my time in Germany. I also met a girl named Suzanne. She would later become my wife. We were married for almost five years. We were total opposites and in the end I think I was trying to marry my awesome experience in Germany through Suzanne. I strayed from my marriage and my vows to Suzanne. I became involved with a new 'chat' service that the internet was offering. I met a woman. We chatted. We cheated. That relationship spelled the end of my marriage. This behavior of starting a new relationship before ending the existing relationship would prove to be my pattern for several years to come.

For the next several years I explored various relationships. Each one had something different to offer, but none of them "Checked all my boxes." That was my way of saying that this person had some of the qualities I wanted, but not all of them.

Fast forward to Sheryl. I remember talking to her on the phone, talking about her problems, her relationships, and life in general. I was very used to the role of 'counselor' when talking to women, especially beautiful women I was attracted to. This had been my lot in life since junior high. I was always great at talking to the 'hotties' but they were always 'hot' for someone else, not a geek boy like me.

I remember that during my time of 'dating the world,' I wanted to go slow with Sheryl, be her friend; my 'date plate' was quite full. We talked on the phone and then we finally met. We met at Mail Boxes Etc on a radio remote; I thought, MAN she is SMOKING HOT! Our first date was Mexican food, at the end, a hug, nothing more.

Sheryl "checked all my boxes," she had everything I wanted, so I thought, "Let's get hooked up, let's get married!" However, our testimony is that God cannot bless sin, and so He could not bless our living together.

So why stray when you have it all? For me, it was a pattern. While being exclusive with Sheryl I would still connect with radio listeners for lunch. Harmless. No big deal, but when you put yourself in dangerous situations, when you 'play with fire', you will get burned. At one lunch, I felt an attraction to another woman. She could not offer AT ALL what Sheryl had, but it seemed like this was the way my life worked, I met someone, we clicked, we dated, then I strayed.

I was now being a jerk to Sheryl, lying about not being sure about getting married, saying "I need time to think, I'll take a drive," only to connect with the other woman. I would tell the other woman, "Yes, I am breaking up with Sheryl, there will be time for us", when I knew that was a lie. I knew I still had strong feelings for Sheryl but was in the pattern of relationship hopping. Part of me wondered why I needed to "hop" again, since Sheryl did "check all my boxes", but "hopping" was the pattern the enemy had me in at the time. I was believing the lie that this pattern was what I was stuck with for the rest of my life.

Finally I felt that God got through my THICK HEAD with a message - "STOP RUNNING! STOP RUNNING FROM ME! BREAK THE PATTERN!" I could see that God had allowed His grace to pour over me during my season of "dating the world." He had protected me from seriously stupid and dangerous behavior and now He was giving me the woman of my dreams but He wanted me to follow Him in order to have Sheryl.

I remember when I was going to tell Sheryl the truth, I felt awful. I was so scared that I would lose her, but I knew that I needed to stop running. God had finally given me the desire of my heart. If anything, the other relationships proved that to me. I had "dated the world" and I TOTALLY knew that Sheryl was the best for me.

The night I finally had the courage to tell Sheryl everything is the "night from Hell." It was a very emotional night but through that pain we began a relationship that was blessed by God. Now we stand as a testimony of the truth - The truth is - (1) God can't bless something done in sin (2) As long as you have breath - you still have a chance to ask for forgiveness and turn your life around.

What I Know Now:

1. There is freedom in truth, even when the truth hurts.

2. You cannot out sin God's grace, mercy, or forgiveness.

3. God allowed me and Doug to almost lose our relationship to gain it.

4. We both needed to work on ourselves emotionally and spiritually.

5. Doug took responsibility for his choices.

6. Doug was the first person in my life who did not make me feel fearful, intimidated, manipulated, or responsible for any of his choices or issues. I did not feel an unhealthy need to help him. He did not need me in that way. These facts are what helped me respond the way I did to the situation. I was able to express myself and we were able to communicate and lay everything on the table. Nothing was swept under the rug. This was a first for me. It was hard but it was worth it. It was a key turning point in our relationship.

Puzzle Piece 17

Second Chances

II Corinthians 5:17
If anyone is in Christ, he is a new creature; the old things passed away; behold, new things have come.

Once the truth was out, once all the cards were on the table, we then had a chance at a new beginning. Ours was going to be a new relationship in many ways for us, individually and together. Doug wanted to pray with me, he wanted to come totally clean. He said he loved me and was so sorry (again those words did not have a whole lot of meaning to me). He was willing to call the counselor and tell him everything. He was willing to come to church with me. He also called his mom and told her everything. He wanted us to have clean slates and make God a part of our relationship. He took a huge leap by confessing to me. I took a huge leap by allowing him to continue to be in my life.

Once we met with Dr. Don things progressed quickly. He helped us walk through this new chapter. Everything came out. No more lies, no more hiding. We talked openly about everything. Doug debated if he should move out so we could keep our new vow of abstinence until marriage. He was determined we would be married as "spiritual virgins." We ended up deciding he would stay in the apartment but sleep on the couch. We were both very sure we wanted to do it all right this time. We wanted God to be first in our relationship. We wanted God at the head. At our next counseling appointment, we decided that we **did** want to get married and we wanted to do it soon. This was not just Doug's decision, with me going along to make him happy because I thought that was what he wanted, it was MY decision also.

We decided to pass on our original wedding date of June 9th and get married the following week - May 22, 1996. Our counselor was also an ordained minister. He married us in the living room of his home, with my best friend Lisa and Doug's best friend Hans by our sides. We also kept our original date and renewed our vows and shared our testimony before family and friends on June 9th.

During our ceremony, Doug wanted us to play the song *This Time* by David Meece. This beautifully written song talks about second chances and moving forward in life. We wanted everyone who attended our wedding to hear our testimony through this song.

We were originally going to have a bridal party but we knew things were now different. Lauren was the only bridal attendant, she became my maid of honor and our flower girl. My dad was very happy for me and willingly flew to California from Alabama just to walk me down the aisle. As Doug entered the room, his mom walked him down the aisle to the song, *Going to the Chapel*. It was no longer the wedding and reception that we had originally planned; it was now about the family I had longed for all my life and as David Meece sings in his song, *This Time*, it was about "second chances with no backward glances," for both of us.

What I Know Now:

1. A relationship with God at the head, based on love, honor, integrity, and grace is a relationship that I am grateful for.

2. There is no such thing as a perfect marriage but choosing to love, honor, and serve one another is a choice we must make daily as husbands and wives.

3. I pray daily that Doug and I will love and serve one another well.

4. Marriage is work. Marriage takes trust. Marriage takes time to build. Marriage is a commitment. Marriage takes communication. Marriage is two people who desire to love, serve, and help each other by being the best they can be to themselves and each other.

Puzzle Piece 18

A New Life

Luke 6:47-49

Everyone who comes to Me and hears My words and acts on them, I will show you whom he is like: he is like a man building a house, who dug deep and laid a foundation on the rock; and when a flood occurred, the torrent burst against that house and could not shake it, because it had been well built. But the one who has heard and has not acted accordingly, is like a man who built a house on the ground without any foundation; and the torrent burst against it and immediately it collapsed, and the ruin of that house was great.

Looking back I can really see how quickly and easily things fell into place after we gave our hearts to Christ. However we still had our struggles and challenges. It did take a lot of time, commitment, and communication to re-build the trust. Actions do speak louder than words. We also agreed to put up boundaries in our interactions with the opposite sex. We still practice these boundaries today. We love Billy

Graham's philosophy. As Dr. Graham does, neither of us goes anywhere with a member of the opposite sex alone. There has to be at least one other person. We respect each other as well as ourselves and do not put ourselves in compromising situations.

Typically when someone strays it is not a planned situation. We do not want to give the enemy a foothold at all, not even a tiny toe. We have also worked very hard to keep our own spiritual armor on. We pray for each other daily. We talk about everything. I work hard at not allowing anything to be swept under the rug. While this can very difficult, it is very important.

As a family we immediately connected at the church I had started attending, Westgate Community Church in San Jose, California. We went every Sunday. Doug and I got involved with a small group. Lauren got involved in the children's program called Awanas. Through this program she came to accept Christ and chose to be baptized. I participated in the women's events. As I began to open up with other women, I saw that even though they all looked perfect on the outside and had the appearance of having it all together, they all had their own stories as well. We all had different stories and backgrounds but I was beginning to see it was not imperative that I was perfect in the eyes of God, nor to these women. I was also beginning to see that God wanted me just as I was.

Very shortly after we made our new commitment to God and to our family, Doug had an opportunity to do the morning show for a Christian radio network outside of Nashville. This move had many meanings for us. At the time things were quiet with my ex-husband, but I never knew when that could change. I did my best to always include him with Lauren's school and church functions but I still feared him. I have never forgotten what he is capable of. I was always afraid if I made him mad he would come after me, or even possibly have someone else do it. I was also afraid that he would try to take

Lauren away from me. He never threatened me with any of those things, nonetheless, I knew he was very capable of doing all of them and more if he wanted. Even though these thoughts were always in my mind, I really did want things to be "ok" for Lauren. I did not want to put her through what I went through as a child. I was always very careful not to tell her anything negative about her dad. The job offer for Doug and the move would put thousands of miles between Lauren's dad and us. I needed my ex-husband's approval to take her out of state. He gave it to me. I was very relieved that God would put so much distance between us.

As things changed with Doug and me so did things between my mom and me. I recently re-read a journal entry in what I call a family history journal and noticed a comment I wrote about my mom right before we knew we were going to move. "It seems like we are never on the same page. I feel like she wants a friend and I want a mom. When I am close to God she backs way off. Things become strange. I sense a lot of fakeness and phoniness. There has always been a distance between us and I don't understand it. I feel like I do not know her. I feel like I have a big puzzle in front of me and I don't have all the pieces yet."

As I continued to try to figure out my relationship with my mom we found out I was pregnant! We were all very excited. Not only would we be moving, but now we would also have a new addition to our family. Shortly after our news of moving and my pregnancy, my mom and stepdad told us they were also going to move to Tennessee. This surprised me. They said they were looking at moving from the high prices of California and wanted to retire in a few years somewhere where the prices were more affordable. Since we were now moving to Tennessee, they thought it would be a good idea to follow and set themselves up for retirement in the future. Unbeknownst to me at the time, this decision would give me several more missing puzzle pieces as the years went by.

In August 1998, two months after we arrived in Nashville, our son Garic was born. I felt very blessed that God allowed me to have another child, a son! Lauren had been anticipating her brother's arrival; she talked to him daily inside my womb. She could not wait to hold and cuddle her baby brother. Doug was thrilled at the thought of having a son. He has always loved Lauren as if she were his very own. He was excited at having the opportunity to raise and love a child from the very beginning as well. I experienced the same overflowing sense of love that I had when my daughter was born 10 years earlier.

No words can adequately describe how a mother feels when she holds her newborn baby for the first time. The moment Garic finally arrived and we heard his healthy cry, Doug and I both cried and hugged one another saying, "We have a son! We have a son!"

When my dad got the call from Doug about our new son, he drove three and a half hours from Alabama to Tennessee. I felt overjoyed at the thought that he was able to be there shortly after Garic was born. Once he arrived and entered my hospital room, I hugged him tightly and thanked him for coming all this way to meet his new grandson. He hugged me back firmly and said, "I wasn't missin' out on this one!"

After we brought our son home and settled in for our new family life, we made it a priority to find a church and get plugged in. We finally settled on Harpeth Heights Baptist Church in Nashville, Tennessee. We were all very active and involved from Sunday service and Sunday school to Wednesday nights. Harpeth Heights is where I first felt my calling from God to share with other women.

I started by leading a Moms In Touch prayer group. Later I led book studies based on the "Bad Girls of the Bible" series by Liz Curtis Higgs. Liz is an amazing woman. I was overwhelmed by her honesty and her own testimony. I felt connected to her. She was so real to me. She walked in similar shoes to mine! I loved how she told the stories of the women of the Bible. She made them real and relatable to me. Hers was a life-changing book for me, and I wanted to share it with anyone who would listen.

With each book we read and discussed, it seemed our "masks" were coming off. It was the first time in my life that I had openly shared my testimony. I was in awe at the other women's response towards me. For once in my life I was seeing my sins not as a scarlet cord around my neck but as a testimony of grace and forgiveness. The scarlet cord represents the blood of Jesus washing over all of my sins, cleansing me of my sin – NOT reminding me of my guilt and shame. This was a huge spiritual turning point in my life. During this time Doug created a similar group for the men. They had Bible study and prayer time. He was also sharing openly about his past. We both recognized the power of taking off our masks and walking in truth.

What I Know Now:

1. Healthy boundaries in a marriage are important. Every couple needs to identify (preferably before you say, "I do.") what your healthy boundaries will be.

2. Boundaries are not always convenient. While it can sometimes be a little awkward with our boundary of not going anywhere alone with a member of the opposite sex, this is an area that is important to both of us. Doug has agreed to this boundary to show respect and honor towards me.

3. Finding a church family and getting involved is important for your spiritual growth.

4. I was still functioning with PTSD in regards my ex-husband.

Puzzle Piece 19

My Dad

Matthew 17:20

He said to them, "Because of the littleness of your faith; for truly I say to you, if you have faith the size of a mustard seed, you will say to this mountain, 'Move from here to there,' and it will move; and nothing will be impossible to you."

I know my dad's in heaven. I also know he died an alcoholic. My dad was never good at communicating. He would rather give you the silent treatment than let you know you had disappointed him, made him mad, or hurt his feelings. That seemed to be easier for him than talking about the situation or dealing with the problem. I have very few memories of him being completely sober. He usually had a beer in his hand by the afternoon. Before his death, he went straight towards the hard stuff and started drinking first thing in the morning. He died suddenly in May of 2000, surrounded by empty alcohol bottles. His last years were filled with severe alcoholism, depression, and grief. When his mother died unexpectedly in 1984, it was emotionally very hard for him.

Though my grandmother had a few health problems, no one suspected that she would soon have a heart attack and die. It happened while she and my grandfather were on a trip from California to Alabama. My dad was devastated that he did not get to say goodbye to her. He was very close to both of his parents, but especially to his mother. After her death, he began to drink more.

After my grandmother died, my dad and grandfather decided to move "home" from California back to Alabama. They moved to Albertville, Alabama and bought two homes within walking distance of each other. In the midst of trying to fill his own personal void with alcohol, my dad started attending church. I think he wanted to, but it is also something that is almost expected in the South. Asking where you attend church is almost as common as asking your name. I think that made it easier for my dad to want to attend. My dad and grandfather drove an hour each way to Birmingham, Alabama, every Sunday morning, to attend Mountain View Baptist Church. That is where his cousin and her family had been going for years. Shortly after they began attending, my dad and grandfather walked down the aisle together as they both had decided they wanted to accept Jesus as their Lord and Savior. I will never forget the phone call my dad made to tell me of his decision. He was excited. I was overjoyed.

A short time later, when my grandfather died of lung cancer, my dad seemed to spiral hard and fast into severe depression. His drinking became even more of a problem, and he never considered reaching out for help or accepting intervention. It was easier for him to reach for the bottle.

After my grandfather passed away, my dad continued to go to church for a while and he even made the decision for baptism. He was very proud of his decision. Someone took a Polaroid picture of the event, and it stayed on my dad's refrigerator until the day we sold his house. Unfortunately, his grief and alcoholism took up more and more of his time and he spent less and less time going to church. While I know he appreciated the phone calls and visits from the pastors and his cousin, he kept all of his pain inside. He never shared his grief or pain.

My dad told me he regretted not making church a part of our family life growing up. Even though he was attending church and had accepted Christ, he was not willing or able to let go of his grief or alcoholism. He held onto both of them tightly. A year before he died I had a very rare visit with him. He was completely sober and we began to talk about his relationship with my mom, my childhood, and his life. We looked through all the old photos that he still had, including the photos of my parents' brief marriage. It always surprised me that he and my grandparents continued to keep all of my parent's photos. I always enjoyed looking at them throughout the years. That particular time, I was trying desperately to see something in their eyes or body language to suggest something other than the truth of their relationship back then. I did not find it.

My dad really opened up to me during that conversation. He was honest enough with me to confess things he did. He took responsibility for his choices and actions. He told me he loved my mom and he was in love with her when they married. He claimed he really did want to make their marriage work. In the end, according to him, it became too hard. Too many things had gone on between them, too many accusations, and too many arguments. In his mind and his heart, it was too late to make it work in the end.

I am grateful that I had the opportunity to talk with my dad. Although the conversation was years later than it should have been, at least I had it. I suddenly had more puzzle pieces to add to my picture.

What I Know Now:

1. Alcoholism is a disease. It robs people of life and relationships.

2. My dad's desire not to confront or deal with heart issues runs deep within his family.

3. I regret not talking to my dad about the molestation accusation towards my ex-husband. We buried it deeply under the rug after he called me and I took Lauren to meet him for the first time.

4. Covering, ignoring, or burying problems or issues before you deal with them does not make them go away. They continue to grow silently.

5. My dad was not perfect but I do believe he did the best he could, the best he knew how. I know he loved me.

Puzzle Piece 20

Lies And The Truth

John 8:32
and you will know the truth, and the truth will make you free.

While Doug and I were enjoying our new life in Nashville, I continued to send Lauren's dad her school papers, report cards, information on field trips, etc. – anything to make him feel like he knew what was going on. For the most part, he remained true to his word to take care of Lauren financially; although, as the years passed, it was harder and harder to get him to keep his word. Visitation was also much harder. She had to fly back and forth versus a simple car ride across town. It started off that she would fly out to see him in the summer for a week and we agreed on every other Christmas or Thanksgiving. Whoever did not have Christmas had her at Thanksgiving. Those visits began to diminish as the years passed by. He made lots of promises and plans, sometimes following through and sometimes not. Whenever she was with him, I always made sure to have daily phone calls from her. I think that was as much for my peace of mind as it was for hers. He was careful not to expose her to much, and he hid things from her.

He ended up marrying for a second time, and even included Lauren in the ceremony. Unfortunately, within a short time Lauren was witness to several violent situations between him and his new bride. He never knew she heard or saw anything. All too often, parents think their kids are not paying attention, but they most certainly are. I am sure lots more went on than she was aware of. That marriage ended in divorce within a matter of years.

Although he lived thousands of miles away, my behavior towards him and fear of him continued. I still would not confront him. I continued to allow things to be swept under the rug with him. One time Lauren came home from a visit, and she mentioned something about how her dad had been a Japanese foreign exchange student in high school. I turned my head, afraid I would laugh aloud. I asked her to tell me what the conversation was about. She said they had gone out to dinner with his then wife and her parents to a Japanese restaurant. He started telling stories of his experience in Japan as an exchange student. I know he was never a foreign exchange student. We went to the same high school and in our nine years together I never saw photos, memorabilia, or heard stories about this. I knew he was lying. He always told outrageous stories, but remained believable to those who did not know the truth. Most people, even if they had a hard time believing what he said, never questioned him. I told Lauren that I would not call her father a liar but I did tell her that to my knowledge he was never a foreign exchange student before he married me or during our marriage. I should have called him at the moment and asked him why he told such a lie. I should have made him tell Lauren the truth. I did not. I continued to stay within the boundaries that he had created. I continued to meet his expectations.

There were a few times over the years that I felt brave enough to confront him, and when that happened the abusive man I knew so well would come out – angry and cursing. He was a master at turning things around and making it my fault. It seemed as if it was easier for him to blame others than to take responsibility. Over time, the visits, promised presents, trips, and the financial support became a cause of disagreement between us.

He promised Lauren many things. He told her not to be afraid to ask for things that she needed or wanted. While he came through at times, more often than not Lauren had to hear incredible stories of how her gifts were stolen or lost in the mail.

Money and child support payments were also an ongoing issue. He said he wanted her to be able to experience as much as she could in high school. When the money was due we always had to front it or ask if we could please pay it later, then hound him (in a very friendly non-threatening way) until he paid it. He also created a pattern of making me responsible for reminding him of the monthly child support check. I dreaded the monthly reminder calls but I played his game because I did not feel I had any choice. This was very stressful to me. Each month, after the agreed upon deadline for payment had passed, I had to make my "friendly" reminder phone call asking him for the support and anything additional he may have told Lauren he would do. I felt I had to talk nice to him and make him feel connected to Lauren still. I gave him the illusion we are "friends." Over the years, I confronted him a few times on late "payments" (after my friendly reminder call) and even asked if it would be helpful to change the due dates. That was always met with anger, and somehow I was at fault again. I counted down the days until Lauren's graduation, all the while thinking, *Once Lauren graduates then I will not have to deal with him anymore. I can just say what I want to say and it will not affect her or me anymore."* The whole time I tried to tell myself that, I continued to live in fear of him. Who was I really kidding? I could never stand up to him.

What I Know Now:

1. I felt trapped in my relationship with my ex-husband even though we had been divorced for several years.

2. Telling lies, outrageous stories, and manipulating people and situations for your own benefit, speaks to a deeper heart issue usually involving low self-esteem, shame, fear, and emotional issues.

3. Confronting someone is never easy but God gave us an example of how to confront others in Matthew 18:15-17. This scripture is talking about confronting other believers within the church, but I believe you can apply the concept to any confrontation.

4. Galatians 6:1 tells us the attitude we should have when confronting others, "Brethren, even if a man is caught in any trespass, you who are spiritual, restore such a one in a spirit of gentleness; each one looking to yourself, lest you too be tempted."

Puzzle Piece 21

More Puzzle Pieces

Psalm 119:105
Your word is a lamp to my feet, and a light to my path.

As life progressed for us in Tennessee, things with my mom really began to heat up. She had one drunken episode that led to us putting up some major, and long needed, boundaries to her behavior. During that alcoholic outburst she asked me if my stepdad and I ever did anything. I was not sure what she meant. She then asked if he had ever touched me or done anything sexual with me. I felt shocked by her question. I looked at her for a moment, searching my mind for any shred of truth to her accusations. To the best of my knowledge and memory, I have never been molested or abused by my stepdad.

I suddenly felt nauseous, light headed, and my heart began to race. I wondered if she had been carrying this around for over fifteen years, and if so, why hadn't she said something sooner? If she suspected it, why hadn't she protected me? How could she have looked me in the eyes if she thought there was anything somehow consensual? Why did she let him around my daughter?

After my mom sobered up, I asked her if I could pray with her. She agreed, and then wanted to go home. We took her home and the next day I received the traditional and expected phone call saying she was sorry and that there would – once again – be no more alcohol in the house.

During the phone call I finally laid down some much-needed boundaries. I told her that the next time she called me to "rescue" her, I would not come alone, and I would bring the police. I encouraged her to seek help. This conversation was a huge turning point in my relationship with my mom. For the most part, the drunken phone calls stopped and I was spurred on to begin to identify and understand unhealthy patterns and behavior in my mom, my ex-husband, and myself. I was beginning to get spiritually and emotionally healthy, and I knew I needed to change things for the benefit of my children and myself.

What I Know Now:

1. Boundaries are helpful and necessary in life.
2. According to Webster's Dictionary the definition of a boundary is "something that marks or fixes a limit".
3. As a visual learner I like to think of healthy boundaries like a cage. If you choose to visit a zoo, most of the animals are in cages. The cages not only protect you from a wild animal but they also protect the animal from those who would want to bring harm to it whether intentional or not.

Puzzle Piece 22

Blessings and Changes

Isaiah 41:10

Do not fear, for I am with you: Do not anxiously look about you, for I am your God I will strengthen you, surely I will help you, Surely I will uphold you with My righteous right hand.

During our first few years in Nashville, we lived just a few minutes from my mom and stepdad. We were renting a large 3-bedroom townhome in Nashville. Doug and I began to talk and pray about buying a home. We had no idea if we could even qualify for a home loan. God opened many doors for us and within a very short time frame, God blessed us with our first home. It was about 30 minutes away from my mom and stepdad, and just minutes away from my husband's job. We were moving to Franklin, Tennessee.

One drawback to our new home in Franklin was the distance it put between our home church and us. Once we moved, we commuted for about a year and a half. As Lauren entered high school we felt the need to find a new church, closer to home. We wanted Lauren to be able to connect to friends at church closer to home. The commute was also getting hard as I was also working at the church preschool during the week while our son Garic was attending the program. Going back and forth five times a week was taking its toll.

After much prayer and the blessing and understanding of our church, we began to search for a new home church closer to us. After much prayer and visiting several churches, we decided on Strong Tower Bible Church in Franklin. This was unlike any church we had attended before. We loved the diversity of the pastors and the congregation. It reminded us of the diversity we had left behind in the San Francisco Bay Area. We also agreed with everything they believed and preached.

We all jumped in and were connected. I felt God leading me towards helping with the youth. This was new to me as I had really loved working with the women's ministry, but I felt it was going to be a new season for me. I helped organize and create the Student Youth Council as well as a youth newsletter. I enjoyed getting to know the youth, and Lauren seemed to like having me involved. I was also volunteering in the children's ministry, helping with the Wednesday night program.

While God blessed us with a new home and we enjoyed spiritual growth at our church, He also challenged us with the loss of Doug's job. The radio station he worked at wanted to change direction with their morning show, and through no fault of his own, he was fired. This is an unfortunate down side to my husband's career. Radio is not a stable career path and things can turn on a dime.

Three years after moving our family across the country, my husband was fired from the Christian radio station that brought us to Tennessee. I was angry. Although Doug and I were – and continue to be – friends with his co-workers and boss, I was carrying around some unhealthy resentment towards the man who fired my husband. Those emotions were hard to contain, as the home we had just purchased was four houses down from his family's home.

Months went by and God's hand remained on us. Miraculously, the purchase of the house was not affected by his job loss. Doug sent résumés and tapes all over the country. I did not want to move. I loved our new home and neighborhood. A few months went by, and during those months we received many anonymous gift cards. There were even a few times when we really should have not gone out to eat a meal, but we did, and someone picked up our tab! This was an amazing testimony to me. Things like this never happened before.

As I struggled with my feelings towards Doug's former boss, God kept working on my heart. For a few years, I had been learning that there is nothing wrong with emotions, even anger, as long as you keep it under control. Along with my newfound understanding, I was also less likely to continue my old practice of sweeping things under the rug. My new goal was to confront things in a Christ like manner, and to deal with them.

One day Lauren and I were walking in our neighborhood when I suddenly realized that we were going to cross paths with "him" – Doug's ex-boss. Although we only lived four houses away from him, I had never seen him walking in the neighborhood before so I was surprised. As we passed one another we did the courtesy nod, said hi, and kept walking. Then I stopped and turned around. I called his name, and walked toward him and said that I needed to ask his forgiveness. I told him that I had been holding onto anger towards him regarding the situation with my husband. He looked at me and said he understood, and told me that his wife would have probably felt the same way. He said I did not need to apologize. Although I really wanted to go into detail and explain myself and justify my feelings and rehash the unfair way I felt my husband was treated, I felt a tug on my heart from God saying, "Just apologize and don't justify it." I told him I appreciated what he said but that I felt I needed to ask forgiveness. He looked at me and said, "OK, Sheryl I forgive you." We smiled at each other and I thanked him. We turned and went our separate ways. I suddenly felt such a huge relief. I was freed from the bondage of anger I had been holding onto. I thank God for that opportunity and for His timing.

The loss of Doug's job was a time for our family to grow in our faith. While we were trying to be open to the idea of moving, we were very thankful when God allowed us to stay in our home. Within three months Doug was offered another job at another local Christian station, 94FM The Fish, where he remains to this day.

What I Know Now:

1. Forgiveness = freedom
2. Forgiveness is a simple yet complex word. It can be hard to ask for and hard to accept. If your heart is in the right place it can also be easy to ask for and easy to accept.
3. Forgiveness can, at times, mean more to the person asking for it than it does to the person receiving it.
4. Jeremiah 29:11 "For I know the plans that I have for you," declares the Lord, "plans for welfare and not for calamity to give you a future and a hope."

Puzzle Piece 23

Give Him the Keys

John 14:27
*Peace I leave with you; My peace I give to you; not
as the world gives do I give to you, Do not let your
heart be troubled, nor let it be fearful.*

As God was stretching and growing me in many areas of
my personal life, I was still really struggling with the issues
related to my mom. I decided to make a counseling
appointment with the women's ministry director at our church,
Kristi McClelland. I told her I felt like I had many scattered
puzzle pieces and I could not put them together. I wanted
things to be different in my relationship with my mom. I
wanted what I felt other women had with their moms. I never
felt I had that. I longed for closeness, real closeness.

While my mom was close geographically, I never felt close
to her emotionally. We did things together and could spend time
together, but there was never the mother-daughter connection I
longed for. I never saw my mom as a stable person. The alcohol
made her a different person. In sober times, she got along well
with my stepdad and things always appeared very positive.

They held hands and would be very affectionate. She would say that he was her best friend. Under the influence, the opposite was true. After she was drinking, she would tell me horrible things about my stepdad, my father, and even things about her first husband. In the midst of her instability, it was impossible for her to be the kind of mom I longed for.

In the beginning of my counseling sessions, Kristi taught me something very important and life changing: I needed to "give the keys" to my husband. I am a visual learner, therefore I quickly began to see a picture in my mind of me intentionally handing my husband a set of keys. The concept behind that phrase reminded me that my husband is my covering. God designed the husband to be the head of the family, and one of his duties is to protect. The whole time, I had been in charge when it came to disruptions from my mom. I had also been the one dealing with my ex-husband. I was not allowing my husband to protect me or take care of me in those areas. I held the keys to those relationships. Whenever something came up with my mom or my ex-husband I always talked to Doug about it, but I never let him step in for me. I never let him confront my mom or my ex-husband when they said or did things that were hurtful or upsetting. Even though I had grown spiritually and emotionally, I still had fears and anxiety issues when it came to confrontations with those two people in my life.

I began to see the benefits of handing my husband the keys. It was a hard thing to see, acknowledge, and change. Once I allowed it to happen a huge burden was lifted up off my shoulders. It took time. I needed to recognize my own attitudes and behavior and then willingly give my husband the "keys." It was also important for me to see how he handled situations. I needed to trust him in this area. The more I gave him the keys, the more it allowed me to slow down, and I began to see some things clearer. Certain puzzle pieces began falling into place.

What I Know Now:

1. "Giving my husband the keys" was the beginning process of my healing.

2. It was easier to give my husband the keys with situations regarding my mom than it was with situations with my ex-husband.

3. Giving your husband the keys is something that takes time, trust, and communication.

4. God created men to be our protectors and providers. Allowing my husband to help me make decisions and to support boundaries that we agreed upon allowed me to come under his covering and allowed him to do what God intended as one of the husband's roles.

Puzzle Piece 24

The Move That Opened The Door

I Chronicles 16:11-12

Seek the LORD and His strength; Seek His face continually. Remember His wonderful deeds which He has done. His marvels and the judgments from His mouth.

While I was finding comfort in the new "give him the keys" concept, God helped me further by putting some distance between my mom and stepdad and the rest of my family. After following us from California to Nashville, all of a sudden they decided to move to another state, thousands of miles away. This decision was, to me at least, sudden and unexpected. After they told us of their plan, it was only a matter of weeks before they left. Shortly after their move, I received a very drunk and emotional phone call from my mom saying my stepdad had left her.

My mom sounded incredibly desperate and scared. She asked my sister and me to please come visit her. She said she would pay for the airfare; we both agreed. Although she remained sober the whole visit, it was very stressful. I was grateful my sister was there with me. With a seven-year age difference between us, she and I had different memories and experiences growing up with my mom. Now, as adults united to help our mom, the visit ended up being a good opportunity for us to reconnect.

My sister and I tried desperately to put the pieces together with our mom. We both wanted finally to know the truth about things that she alluded to during her drunken rants. Was my stepdad really a controlling mean person? Did he cheat on her? Did he abuse her?

My sister and I pressed her to give us examples of the behaviors that she has always eluded to. The two things my mom used as examples, regarding his controlling nature, were that he was in charge of the TV remote and she never got to watch any shows she wanted, and if she took something out for dinner that he did not really want she would have to put it back and eat whatever it was he wanted. She also insisted he was a complete and total womanizer. She claimed he flirted openly with bank tellers, grocery clerks, and waitresses. She also said he openly fondled women's breasts, the same bank tellers, grocery clerks, waitresses that he flirts with in public. When we questioned her about this, asking why all these women would allow him to do this in her presence, let alone be treated that way period, she said, "Because they all liked it."

This raised some huge red flags for me. In all the years I have known my stepdad (since I was six) I never ever heard or saw him act in any way inappropriate or flirtatious towards any woman. If he was the controlling womanizer that my mom claimed he was, then he did an amazing job of concealing it to me. I returned home, sad for mom, but happy that I had connected with my younger sister, and very confused about my mom and stepdad's life together.

After reestablishing himself back in Nashville, my stepdad called me to announce his return. He was very hesitant on the phone. He was not sure where he stood with me. It was obvious he and my mom had many issues between them. He struggled with guilt and shame about not being able to control the situation. He and my mom were masters of sweeping things under the rug and not dealing directly with them. It had apparently come to a head during their last very intense argument.

My mom did not like being alone. In fact, since her first marriage at the age of fifteen, she had *never* been alone. A few months after my stepdad returned to Nashville, my mom decided she also wanted to come back to Tennessee. She had become very paranoid without my stepdad there to help her maintain stability. She was convinced that she was being followed, that her phone was tapped, and that people were out to get her. She was scared and lonely. She wanted to move back to Nashville, but not to reconcile with my stepdad. To this day, they are still separated.

I began to recognize patterns. My mom and stepdad always moved around a lot, city-to-city, state-to-state, or just apartment-to-apartment, and it was always because of someone or something else. My mom left jobs because of someone else's behavior or something that was done to her. Were these things all due to other people, my mom, my stepdad, or a combination of everyone? Neither of them had consistent or long term friendships. The one person that I knew my mom to be friends with, when I was in high school, she suddenly dropped without confronting the woman about the reason why. It was as if they were both searching for a better place or situation and were always looking for the negative in the situation or in the person. Waiting for the moment to be hurt or taken advantage of. Again I wondered, was this my mom or my stepdad or a combination of both?

Before moving on, I feel the need to remind you that my story is true. If you have never lived with alcoholic parents or been in an abusive relationship, some parts of my story might sound unbelievable. I promise all the things I have said are true. Now hold on because things are really going to get crazy.

What I Know Now:

1. The relationship my mom and stepdad had was very complicated and I may never fully understand it.
2. I have never stopped loving, caring, or praying for both of them.
3. I pray that my mom and stepdad truly seek God with their hearts, souls, and minds. Psalm 9:10 says, "And those who know thy name will put their trust in thee; for Thou, O Lord, hast not forsaken those who seek thee."

Puzzle Piece 25

More...

Psalm 27:13-14
I would have despaired unless I had believed that I would see the goodness of the LORD In the land of the living. Wait for the LORD; Be strong and let your heart take courage; Yes, wait for the LORD.

Once my mom moved back to Nashville, she began to change drastically. She began to use words and phrases I never heard her say before. She started cussing and used the "F" word frequently. She lost a lot of weight and started wearing tight jeans and low cut tops. She got a tattoo. She started making friends with young adults in their 20's. She began to drink A LOT more. There were no more apologies after drunken phone calls and no more promises to not have any more alcohol in the house. We suspected she was using drugs. She began dating a man my age who was a serious alcoholic and I suspect a drug addict. He lived with his mother and did not have a job or a driver's license. According to my mom, his mother hated my mother. The few stories my mom told me of their relationship and how they had to sneak around made it sound as if they were two teenagers who were in love but their parents would not allow it.

During this time she also connected with two young men from her work. I do not know much about them. According to her, they told her after becoming fast friends with them, that they had a plan to make her their number one prostitute in a known red-light district in Nashville. Whether they really said this or not, I will never know. She became convinced that her young boyfriend was in on their plan as well. She decided to get him so drunk and so high on crack that he would confess to her. He never confessed, but he did pass out from the amount of alcohol and the crack they smoked.

She panicked thinking he might have overdosed, and called 911. Despite being carried down four flights of stairs strapped to a gurney, he never regained consciousness until hours later at the hospital. After her attempt to extract the truth from him, my mom told us that her boyfriend had confessed his part in the plot on her answering machine. I was anxious to hear this message and finally find one shred of truth to back up my mom's outrageous story.

It should come as no surprise that this message did not contain anything remotely related to the alleged prostitution ring. All that was said on the message was, "What happened? Where is my jacket? We got to talk, man. When can I see you? I do not know what happened. I need my jacket back. Call me back."

From that moment on, she became completely paranoid that her apartment was bugged with video and audio surveillance. She lived in fear that two young men from her work were videotaping her and just waiting to force her into prostitution. At her request, Doug and I went over to her apartment and poured over each and every hole in her stucco ceiling and walls. She had us putty up the smallest of holes with toothpaste. We did what we could to placate her, but there were no holes, no cameras, and no recording devices. There was nothing, nothing at all. But facts have little effect on someone so very paranoid.

She was still convinced her boyfriend was in on the plan with the two young men from her work, so she broke off her relationship with the younger man and sought an order of protection from him. We went to court with her to get her restraining order. I remember being nervous as we entered the courtroom. When I saw him I felt genuine sadness for him. He was my age but looked a lot older. He looked very haggard and worn out. His mother was also there. She struck me as an older woman who was neatly dressed and had a permanent scowl on her face. It was obvious she did NOT like my mother. I think the restraining order made everyone happy.

All the drama that my mom was ensnared in propelled her to want to move again. She decided she wanted to go back to the far off state she just left, and did. During all that drama, I was able to allow my husband to be my protector. He "had the keys" and whenever my mom called, he answered first. Every call was monitored. Often we would let voicemail get it. If she sounded sober I would call her back. If not, I would ignore it. At times, she would get very drunk and make the rounds of phone calls: first to my step dad, then to my sister, then finally to me if she was not satisfied with their calls. And I have no doubt that she would then call other family or friends until they eventually put a stop to it as well.

I remember one time she called and I was sound asleep and accidentally answered the phone. It did not take long to realize she was drunk. I told her I was tired and had to work in the morning, and that I was sorry but I could not continue the conversation at that time. She was so angry that she actually hung up on me. Within seconds she called back. I woke Doug up and he told her that we were sleeping and if she needed emergency help she should call the police. Then she said, "Oh, sorry to bother you," and hung up.

My boundaries were up and it did not take my mom very long to realize that in order to speak to me she had to go through my husband first. As a result, the calls came less frequently. When she did call and leave a sober message, I called her back, with Doug right there in the room, ready to take the phone if she started sounding drunk or angry. That is still our practice to this day.

I do not know if my mom has sought treatment or if she is just careful not to call us anymore when she is drunk. If she *has* sought any kind of treatment she has not shared that with me. I know that things have definitely become quieter. The boundaries I have in place have helped me have less anxiety and worry about my mom. I cannot deal with her until she deals with her addictions and emotional issues. Both of these issues, I believe run deep within her. I do love my mom. I do hope and pray for her daily. I know that God is in control and I have not given up on her, but I cannot give her the help that she needs. I cannot save her. She needs to make those choices herself.

What I Know Now:

1. No matter how Doug and I felt about my mom's situation, I knew it was real to her. That is why we try to help her as best we can while keeping our boundaries in place.

2. In order for me to accept the relationship that I have with my mom I had to grieve the loss of the relationship I desired.

3. I pray that someday my mom will accept the help she needs to deal with her addictions and emotional issues.

4. No amount of indulgent behavior will change your situation or ease your pain. It will more than likely ruin relationships and create more problems for you.

5. There is always hope. Isaiah 43:25 "I, even I, am the one who wipes out your transgressions for My own sake. And I will not remember your sins."

Puzzle Piece 26

Lauren

Zechariah 8:16-17

"These are the things which you should do: speak the truth to one another; judge with truth and judgment for peace in your gates. Also let none of you devise evil in your heart against another, and do not love perjury; for all these are what I hate," declares the LORD.

While we were working through new boundaries with my mom, we were also getting closer to my daughter's graduation from high school in May 2006. As spring arrived and plans for her ceremony and party were underway, I was silently stressing out. I was so worried about having her dad at the graduation party knowing my sister, that he was accused of molesting, would also be there. Lauren knew nothing of the accusations. I did not want to ruin her big day, but I also did not want to disrespect my sister.

Lauren's upcoming graduation opened the door for me to have a much needed, long-overdue conversation with my sister, Shelli. It was a hard conversation. I finally asked her to forgive me for not protecting her from my ex-husband. She forgave me. She said she had forgiven me years ago. We talked about everything, from the first time he touched her inappropriately, to the day she and my dad told me. There were many tears shed. I truly regret allowing that situation to be pushed under the rug for so long. I believe that not talking about it with anyone except my husband contributed to it's holding me captive for so long. The conversation with Shelli helped me arrange a few more pieces of my puzzle. It has only been recently, while on this journey of writing, that I have been able to forgive myself. While I know I have forgiveness, I know the pain of regret is always there.

As it got closer to Lauren's high school graduation, I sent her dad an email telling him that my sister and family would be there. I was mentally preparing to send him another email telling him that he would not be welcome at our home for the party after the ceremony. He could certainly come to the graduation and see Lauren either before or after our party, but he could not come to our home. I never had to send the email. After receiving my first email he started back-peddling, saying he was not sure he could even make it out.

Lauren's dad had already begun to pull away during her senior year, not showing up for her graduation would surely put more distance between them. I wanted to confront him about that. I had not completely given my husband the keys in that relationship yet, and so I was still struggling and holding onto the anxiety of it all. Suddenly Lauren's dad dropped a bombshell on us. He said he was sick with Parkinson's Disease. When I pressed for details or information, he was very vague. I honestly felt like it would end up being his ultimate excuse. While there was a small part of me that wondered if his story could be true, I doubted it was. He was a master storyteller and he had seemed to be looking for a good reason not to come to Lauren's graduation and in my opinion, not to be around my sister. His news was supposed to be the ultimate excuse for his behavior over the previous year.

As the days progressed, he sent Lauren a text message to say he could not attend due to his health issues. On the night of the graduation, he sent her a text to say "Congratulations." Not a card, not an actual phone call, just a simple text. This hurt Lauren deeply. Even though I had felt tremendous relief that he was not coming, I felt the pain Lauren was experiencing at not having her dad genuinely acknowledge her biggest accomplishment at this point in her life. With her graduation, all contact and financial support suddenly came to an abrupt halt. Phone calls were not returned, emails not responded to, text messages ignored, certified letters sent to him, returned. It was as if he just dropped off the face of the earth. I was very sad for Lauren, but selfishly I was relieved for me.

This situation also opened a door for Lauren to seek counseling and it spurred me on to have a real heart to heart talk with her about everything. Much she already knew or had pieced together on her own over the years. The hardest thing to talk about with her was the situation with my sister Shelli. I felt I needed to tell Lauren, since I had realized when I spoke with my sister that her oldest son knew about it. I did not want Lauren to hear it from anyone else, she needed to hear it from me. I also needed to get it out from under the rug. Our conversation was another opportunity to piece together a few more parts of my puzzle.

Following our heart-to-heart in the summer of 2006, Lauren was getting ready to start college in the fall. Even though the college was less than 90 minutes from where we lived, the idea of her being away from home was hard for me. But I knew it was part of her growing up. I struggled through the first few months. I tried to put on the brave mom face when I was around others, but then, at night, when everyone was asleep, I would go and lay on her bed and cry and pray.

Within weeks of Lauren's starting college, she met a boy and instantly jumped into a very serious relationship with him. This caused me great concern and worry. I knew immediately that it would not be a healthy relationship, something in me knew it was not right. The very first time I actually met him I was burdened because I saw so much of her dad in him. Although I did not see his anger or violence, I saw his need to always have a big story. He also seemed to always be the victim. Like her dad, nothing was his fault. He claimed he was a Christian, but there was not any fruit in his life. He said he did not need to do Bible studies or devotion because "I already read the Bible once." He claimed to know the Word but could never articulate anything.

Doug and I saw many red flags, but Lauren was determined to make it work. It was the first real relationship Lauren had been in. He was the first boy she had kissed. She tried her best to make him look good to us. We invited him over for dinner and he tagged along on various family outings. Each time I would pray that God would help me see him thru His eyes and not my own. I never had a peace about him. I was feeling very anxious and afraid for Lauren. When you have walked in the shoes I have, you fight to make sure your child does not make the same mistakes. While my faith was strong and I knew God was bigger than any situation, I still did not want her to put one toe into one my shoes.

<u>What I Know Now:</u>

1. I am very grateful that my sister and I finally "lifted the rug" and talked openly and honestly. It was very hard and even uncomfortable but it was necessary for me to have that conversation in order to move forward.

2. Adjusting to life as your child leaves the nest – whether they go to college or just move out of the house – is a big adjustment.

3. Encouraging and allowing your college-age child to move forward in life is necessary and important for their growth and maturity. It is not always easy though.

4. As a parent of a college-age student or adult child, you can, at times, feel helpless as you watch them make choices that you know are not in their best interest.

5. It is important to keep communication lines open.

6. **Never** stop praying, **never** stop asking questions, **and never** give up.

7. I Peter 5:7 says, "cast all your anxiety upon Him because He cares for you."

Puzzle Piece 27

Panic and Fear

Isaiah 43:2

*When you pass through the waters, I will be with you;
And through the rivers, they will not overflow you.
When you walk through the fire, you will not be
scorched, Nor will the flame burn you.*

December 2006. Lauren was home for Christmas break. It
was close to midnight. Doug, Garic, and I were asleep. Lauren
was in the front room watching TV, when she came running to
my room and said "MOM, GET UP! SOMEONE IS AT THE
FRONT DOOR BANGING AND SCREAMING YOUR
NAME!." I flew out of bed, not fully conscious that Doug
was home. I bumped into the china cabinet as I was trying to
run to the front door, which left a HUGE painful bruise on my
thigh for weeks. I heard a woman crying, saying, "Sheryl help
me! Sheryl help me!" I looked out the peephole on the front
door but I could not see anyone. The woman sounded similar
to my mom. Panic arose in me. My mom was thousands of
miles away, and I knew if it was her then this was going to be

a huge drama. I was scared. I was not going to open the door until I could see who it was.

I suddenly heard someone banging on my son's bedroom window. I ran to look out the window, but I did not see anyone. I could still hear someone crying for me. I ran back to the front door. I was *not* going to open the door until I knew who it was. I was terrified! Each time I went to the door, she went to the window, when I ran to the window, she went back to the door. I remember telling Lauren to get the phone and I called 911. About this time, Doug woke up and came out of the bedroom. I looked at him very confused and I asked him, "When did you get home?" I did not even realize he had been in the bed this whole time. I frantically called 911 and told the operator what was going on. I looked out of the peephole one more time. I saw her now! I told the operator, "I think it's my neighbor but I am not sure."

My neighbor worked in the adult entertainment industry. I knew she was involved with pornographic websites. Everyone knew what she did, but she thought we did not. Up to this point I had been friendly towards her and even brought her food when she had been sick. I tried to minister to her without judging her. She never acknowledged her real job and even lied to us about it in a later phone call. I never told her I knew the truth about her.

I thought the 911 operator told me to open the door and tell her the police were on the way. I snapped! I threw the phone at Doug, put my back to the door firmly, and said, "I can't open the door! I can't open the door!" Doug was trying to tell me that I did not need to open the door, just tell her that help is on the way. I looked thru the peephole and she was standing on the porch, I yelled, "The police are on the way!" She said, "OK" and walked back to her house. We watched thru the peephole and window as several police cars quickly arrived. After approximately 30 minutes, we went outside after we saw an officer standing near our lawn. We noticed a pair of stiletto heels on our lawn near the porch steps. I took them to the officer and said. "I think these belong to my neighbor." Doug asked the police officer what was going on. The officer told us that our neighbor said she had been attacked and robbed by a couple that she had invited into her home.

The next day we saw her and asked if she was ok. She said she was sorry and apologized for scaring us. I told her I was sorry I did not open the door. I was not sure who it was and I was very scared. She told us after the attack the couple drove off and she realized her purse was in their vehicle. Her cell phone was in her purse. She does not have a landline and that is why she came to our home. She wanted us to call the police. Little did I know that God was going to use this experience to cause me to deal with several puzzle pieces of my past.

What I Know Now:

1. I do not want to judge others by their lifestyle, but at the same time I can still be honest about the situation.
2. I was trying to find the balance between loving the sinner and hating the sin. I did not want to judge my neighbor because of her choices. Who among us is sinless?
3. I struggled with letting my neighbor know that I knew the truth about her. That put me back into familiar patterns that I was no longer comfortable with, but I didn't know what else to do.

Puzzle Piece 28

Storm Clouds Gather

Psalm 23

*The LORD is my shepherd, I shall not want. He
makes me lie down in green pastures; He leads me
beside quiet waters. He restores my soul; He guides
me in the paths of righteousness For His name's
sake. Even though I walk through the valley of the
shadow of death, I fear no evil, for You are with me;
Your rod and Your staff, they comfort me. You prepare
a table before me in the presence of my enemies; You
have anointed my head with oil; My cup overflows.
Surely goodness and loving-kindness will follow me
all the days of my life, And I will dwell in the house of
the LORD forever.*

Unbeknownst to me, my life was going to take a huge turn.
I had no idea how my neighbor's incident, as well as the new
freedom I felt from no communication with my ex-husband,
would begin the process of allowing my brain to work through
and unpack a lifetime of situations and events. It had been
eight months since my last contact with Lauren's dad. I found

out from other family and friends that he had been systematically cutting off contact with everyone. Lauren was apparently the last one. We also found out that he had been in a drug and alcohol program several years earlier. I had a strong feeling his lack of contact towards Lauren had to do more with a current drug and alcohol problem than a diagnosis of Parkinson's as he wanted us to believe.

Only in hindsight can I see God's hand over all these things. It was His perfect timing, not mine, for my "storm," and the ultimate healing that would take place emotionally and spiritually but it needed a spark to start. My neighbor's situation was the spark. It brought back memories I had conveniently pushed under the rug. I never forgot them, I just ignored them, and now they came rushing back.

The pounding on my door in the middle of the night reminded me of the time I sought help from a neighbor when my ex-husband beat me. I had always told myself if a woman ever came knocking or pounding on my door for help, I would always help her. I struggled with guilt for not opening the door. I needed to protect my family. I had to realize that I did help her. I called the police, and that was the best thing I could have done for her.

Seeing and feeling the huge bruise on my thigh from bumping into the china cabinet that night (something I had never done before or since), reminded me of my own bruises from past abuse.

The odd relationship with my neighbor – knowing her secrets, but pretending I did not – I camouflaged it with acts of service and compassion for her. I know there is balance between compassion and honesty, but I had conveniently allowed myself to fall back into old habits with her. I went out of my way to make *her* feel comfortable, no matter how uncomfortable *I* was.

I now know why God allowed her to be my neighbor. He allowed her to be there for the purpose of triggering me. It had to happen that way. The reminder of past abuse plus the comfort of not hearing from my ex-husband and allowing myself to fall back into non-confrontational unhealthy patterns, worked together to allow my brain to begin to process what I had been suppressing for too long. It was as if my brain said, "OK, Sheryl you are in a safe place now. Let's deal with this puzzle once and for all." It took almost a month for the storm to arrive.

There was something else that was also going on in the time before my storm hit. Lauren's relationship with her boyfriend was moving along at a fast pace. Doug and I tried very hard to like him. We wanted to see the good in him. I prayed for him daily. Each time I prayed it was as if God was showing us more and more reason to pray "against" him. We were preparing to tell Lauren that we would no longer support their relationship. The young man would no longer be welcome in our home. She of course always would be, but not with him. We had caught him in several lies and felt that he had put Lauren in dangerous situations on more than one occasion. He had also created a pattern of keeping her all to himself. She had slowly let go of friends and activities that she loved. All of her time was being spent with him, alone. We never got the chance to tell her our decision or our reasons. Three days before we had planned to talk with her, I was in the ER.

What I Know Now:

1. God's timing is not always our timing, but it's the best timing.
2. Ecclesiastes 3:1 "There is an appointed time for everything. And there is a time for every event under heaven."
3. Tough love is hard.
4. Red flags almost never change color.
5. I felt powerless to change my daughters' mind about her boyfriend. The reality is that I *was* powerless. It had to be her choice. I had to continue to pray that God would open her eyes and heart to the truth.

Puzzle Piece 29

The Storm Hits

Romans 8:38-39

For I am convinced that neither death, nor life, nor angels, nor principalities, nor things present, nor things to come, nor powers, nor height, nor depth, nor any other created thing, will be able to separate us from the love of God, which is in Christ Jesus our Lord.

January 27, 2007 - 12:30 am. I woke up from a deep sleep feeling very nauseous. I thought I must have been coming down with the flu. I got out of bed to go to the bathroom and felt more nauseous and sudden hot flashes from my neck to my groin. I felt my heart rate speed up. I felt like I could hardly breathe. I thought I was psyching myself out as I have only thrown up one time in my adult life. Maybe I was scared to throw up. I tried to calm down. I went to lie back down as the nausea seemed to subside a little. All the sudden a HUGE wave of nausea hit me with a huge hot flash running from my neck to my groin. My heart was pounding so hard I thought it would pound out of my chest. My chest hurt. I was so scared I could barely breathe. I remember touching Doug and trying to tell him I was sick. He woke up instantly. I then had a BIGGER wave of all the symptoms. I was scared. I knew I was dying.

I felt I could only whisper, as if talking in a normal voice would push me over an edge somehow. I whispered, "Call 911!" He said, "Are you sure?" I whispered, "Yes." He immediately dialed 911. Within minutes an ambulance along with the fire department arrived. They put me on a gurney. I was thinking, "I won't be able to say goodbye to the kids. Lauren is away at college and Garic is still asleep." Doug promised to get Garic up and meet us at the hospital. He was frantically praying the whole way. I remember having several more attacks on the way to the hospital. I did not want to die in the ambulance.

Once we arrived at the hospital, I was given an IV and medication. Even with the medicine, they were only able to bring my heart rate down to 140. A normal heart range is 70-100. I remember praying, and asking God to please let me live. I told Him I would be a better Christian to my family and friends. I wanted to grow old. I wanted grandchildren! Please God, let me be ok.

Doug and Garic arrived within minutes of my arrival. I told Doug to call Lauren. I told him to please tell her I love her. I told him several things just in case I really was dying. I really felt like I was. I told Garic not to be afraid and how much I loved him. I remember Doug and Garic praying over me. It was a time in my life I will never forget.

After many tests, EKGs, X-rays, and a treadmill stress test, the only thing they could find wrong was that I had low potassium. I was given a potassium pill and anxiety medications and sent home to follow up with my family doctor. My family doctor did see me briefly before I was discharged, and commented that she thought I had a panic attack. I remember almost laughing at that. I knew I was not panicking. I knew there was something wrong with me. I could be a worrywart, but I had never had symptoms like those before. No, I was sure it was NOT a panic attack.

What I Know Now:

1. Panic attacks are real.

2. Panic attacks can make you feel like you are dying.

3. Even though I "bargained" with God that I would be a better Christian if He allowed me to live, that was not necessary. We do not need to bargain with God. I know that it was normal to feel that way and that God understood my fears. After all, He knows me better than anyone else.

4. How long we live and whether or not we have physical or mental health problems are not reflections of how good we have been or could be. We will never be *good enough.* That is why we have grace and why Jesus willingly scarified himself on the cross.

5. Isaiah 53:5 states, "But He was pierced through for our transgressions, He was crushed for our iniquities; The chastening for our well-being fell upon Him, And by His scourging we are healed."

6. None of us deserve what Christ did for us. None of us can ever earn this. It is a gift from God. God longs for a relationship with us. We don't have to bargain to get it.

7. The healing mentioned in the verse does not mean we are guaranteed a healthy life. As my pastor once said in a sermon, "Greater is our need to be healed spiritually than a physical healing." I do believe God can and has done physical healing, but if God's will is not to heal you that does not mean you have done something wrong. As my pastor says, "When you are praying for yourself or someone else you should always pray with boldness, faith, hope, and submission to God's will."

Puzzle Piece 30

Let the Healing Begin

Jeremiah 17:14

*Heal me, O LORD, and I will be healed; Save me and
I will be saved, For You are my praise*

Once we were home from the hospital, I followed up with
my family doctor and she gave me an anti-depressant, which I
reluctantly took. She was still insistent that I had a panic
attack. I did not feel "depressed" and I did not understand why
she wanted me to take an anti-depressant. I also still did not
believe I had a panic attack.

I ended up having several more big panic attacks, which
led to another ambulance ride, three ER visits, and many more
tests and several other doctor visits. Finally at the last ER visit,
a nurse thought my symptoms sounded like it could be a panic
or anxiety attack. She told us how one of her family members
had similar symptoms and how they saw a doctor who worked
with them to help. After fighting the diagnosis for so long, I
finally felt like it was worth looking into. I told Doug I wanted
to pray about it. Maybe there was more to this panic and
anxiety than I realized.

I knew if I was going to look into it I wanted to see a woman doctor who was also a Christian. Through a referral I connected with my first psychiatrist, Dr. Anne Fotrell. I cannot say enough about Dr. Anne. She is an amazing doctor. I immediately loved her. She was very familiar with panic and anxiety attacks. She helped me to understand that our brain is a powerful tool. It protects us and at times shields us from dealing with issues that are traumatic, stressful, or emotional. There comes a time though, God willing you live long enough, that your brain will allow you to deal with all the things that, like in my case, were put under the rug. This usually happens when you feel safe and/or something big triggers you. That is what happened to me. As I look back throughout my entire life, I see early signs of panic and anxiety in me. I also know the moment my brain felt safest, when my ex-husband seemed to disappear from our lives. That period is also when my neighbor's situation triggered me. Not everyone will have a severe panic attack like the one I did. It might be smaller. It might come out in a different way; emotionally as depression, or it could be an illness.

In my naiveté, I asked Dr. Anne how long she thought I might need to be on medication and therapy. I was hoping she would say, "Maybe a few weeks." Her response made me realize the issue IS much bigger than I thought. She could not give me an answer, or a time line. Each person is different. Each person responds to medication and therapy in different ways. Part of the answer to my question would also depend on me. I decided immediately that I would pursue healing with a passion. I wanted to be better. I wanted to move forward. I wanted to pull everything out from under the rug and deal with it. I knew it would be hard work, but I was ready to finally deal with everything.

I felt God allowed the door to be opened for a reason, so I wanted to walk through it. Dr. Anne opened my eyes to panic and anxiety and diagnosed me with PTSD (Post Traumatic

Stress Disorder). I was given a different anti-depressant that I took for almost nine months. I also had panic and anxiety medication to help when I had the attacks. She continued to work with me for about seven months. I dragged everything from under the rug and with her help began to sort through it piece by piece. This was emotionally draining, but it was necessary.

A few months into seeing Dr. Anne I was feeling noticeably better. The panic attacks were less frequent and when they did happen they were less intense. She helped me unpack a lot of my past. She helped me work through it. It was really hard for me to talk about everything. I had been very good at putting things under the rug and just moving forward and never dealing with them.

Dr. Anne then felt like the next level of treatment for me would be EMDR (Eye Movement Desensitization and Reprocessing). My initial reaction, when she told me about that type of therapy, was that it sounded a little hokey, but I trusted Dr. Anne and knew that she was very familiar with EMDR and the results it could have. She told me it has been around for over twenty years and that it has proven helpful for people who have had trauma in their lives. She felt very confident that I would benefit from the therapy. I immediately set up an appointment with the doctor she recommended. Dr. Dawne Kimbrell.

I started seeing Dr. Dawne in September 2007. I am very grateful for Dr. Dawne. I have great respect for her and her work with me. While I cannot fully explain how the therapy works. I KNOW it is working. EMDR reprocesses traumatic or stressful memories. It doesn't erase them, but it does help you to process them differently so that you will not be triggered with panic, anxiety, or fears. It has been a hard journey. I have done a lot more "unpacking." It has not been an easy road. I know this writing is also part of the healing that EMDR has given me. I never could have been able to put these things down on paper and see them so clearly without fear and panic rising up in me, had it not been for EMDR. My therapy has helped me look at my life and my past objectively and see why certain things happened the way they did. I can now recognize why I responded to certain things the way I did. I have gained insight into some of the choices I made. Through EMDR I have even been able to see "that girl" (the person I was) and have compassion for "her."

Doctor Dawne has also helped me create a "basket of tools" which I can use to help me when I am facing an anxious or stressful moment. Some of these tools may also be helpful to you.

1. Breathing…. deep breaths in and out.
2. Remove myself from the situation, even if it's around the corner for just a moment. Close my eyes and breathe.
3. Peppermint! My symptoms always start in my stomach with nausea. Peppermint is amazing!
4. Ginger tea… I keep ginger tea bags on hand at all times. I breathe in the smell of the tea and slowly sip it, feeling the sensation of the warm tea going down my throat trying to focus on this sensation rather than my anxiety.
5. Slow down and listen to the sounds around me.
6. Keep hydrated… I always keep a water bottle near me.
7. Take a few moments, when needed, to just sit down in a quiet room and close my eyes (even just a few minutes can make a huge difference).
8. Be aware of trigger points. My triggers are movies, books, or newspaper articles that deal with mental, verbal, or physical abuse or violence. Some things bother me more than others. I have to be aware of how my mind and body are reacting to it. I have asked my husband to keep me accountable when it comes to what we watch on TV, especially the news and traumatic true life stories.

9. Prayer and reading the Bible. I also write scriptures on index cards and post them on mirrors or cupboards.

10. Physical touch. A hug or hand squeeze (even texture- a soft blanket, a fluffy pillow).

11. Keep a journal. Writing things down has really helped me: thoughts, feelings, memories, prayers, etc.

12. Listen to soft instrumental music.

13. Communication. Always talk things over. I work hard at not letting things fester or get pushed under the rug.

14. Acknowledge the choices I have. Maybe I can't change the situation but I can choose how I handle it, if I stay in it, and what I want to do about it

15. Medication. Medication was very helpful for me in the beginning of this crisis, but now it is a very rare moment when I need it anymore.

I have learned there is no quick fix. It takes time and commitment. It truly is one day at a time, which is challenging for me since I want to rush to the finish line. It is also important to find the right doctor and treatment plan. I was very fortunate to connect with my doctors. I know others who were not as fortunate. I would encourage anyone who is looking for a doctor or counselor to make sure there is a connection. Make sure the therapy and treatment plan is something that will work for you. If not, then it is OK to continue to search. This is your mental health. Be your own advocate. You matter!

I have found that psychiatrists, counselors, and doctors all have the same goal in mind – to help the patient – but have discovered that mental health providers are just like the school system, where there are many different types of schools: public, private, religious, home school, etc. There are also many different types of mental health providers. Each provider offers different ideas and styles, but the ultimate goal is the same. Just as each of us has a different learning style, we all respond to people, doctors, and treatments differently. Do not give up until you find what works for you.

Along with all that I am learning about my mental health I am also continuing to learn and grow spiritually. God can use many different things to heal and help us but ultimately all healing comes from Him. Over the years I have seen the importance of regular time in His word and in prayer. Along with connecting with the right doctor, I greatly encourage you to connect daily with God.

I also firmly believe in being involved in church and going regularly, participating as much as possible. Do not worry about finding the perfect church, because it does not exist. Once God leads you to a local church, take the next step. Join. Serve. Serving in church is important, we need to connect and grow with other believers. A stand-alone Christian is an easy target for the enemy.

Also I find having accountability with other women, as well as with my husband, is very valuable. Finding at least one true friend that you can be completely honest with and that will speak the truth in love to you is priceless.

Finally, pursue God with all your heart. Never stop desiring to grow spiritually. It is one step at a time and one day at a time. Read His word. Memorize His promises. Stand on them.

What I Know Now:

1. The tools I listed may or may not work for you. I share these with you to give you an idea of tools that are in my own tool basket.

2. As I have learned more about myself, my triggers, and how my body responds there have been times when I have tried all of my tools and ended up taking medication to ease the panic attack.

3. I will always have panic and anxiety, but as my husband reminded me, "It will never be like it was in the beginning." Dr. Anne once said, "you can never unlearn what you have learned."

4. I believe God can use doctors and medication to help or heal.

5. Isaiah 12:2 says, "Behold God is my salvation, I will trust and not be afraid; for the Lord God is my strength and song, and He has become my salvation."

Puzzle Piece 31

The Healing Continues...
The Puzzle is Complete

Psalm 147:5
Great is our Lord and abundant in strength; His understanding is infinite.

I cannot call this chapter "Healed" because I believe we are never fully healed while we are still here on Earth. Our complete healing happens in Heaven. No more tears, no more sorrows. Until then we press on toward the goal that Christ called us to. I can now apply what God has revealed to me to help myself and help others.

Thanks to my therapy, my two doctors, and all that God has taught me, I can now put my puzzle together. Each piece of the puzzle represents something or someone in my life. The picture in the end was not at all what I thought it would be. It is even better. It is a picture of a beautiful sparrow, soaring high in the blue sky, within its beak is a scarlet cord, flowing in the breeze. The sparrow represents freedom from the past and a look towards today. The sparrow is a bird that no matter how far it goes, always returns home.

At first in my life, the scarlet cord represented all my sin, shame, and guilt. Now that same scarlet cord stands for the blood that Christ shed to pay for all my sin, shame, and guilt. The scarlet cord cannot be discarded, even though it no longer represents what it did at one time, it will be carefully and skillfully woven within the nest of the sparrow. The scarlet cord will now be a symbol of hope and a part of my firm foundation in Christ.

What I Know Now:

1. There is always hope.
2. It is never too late.
3. Once I had all my puzzle pieces out and finally put it together, a huge burden was lifted off my shoulders. Having my puzzle put together and wearing my scarlet cord as a sign of hope and foundation does not guarantee a happily-ever-after life for me. Life is still life, but I do know that I am different. I am more like the woman God desired for me to be the moment I was conceived. I also know God is with me every step of the way.

Puzzle Piece 32

Epilogue....

Ecclesiastes 7:8
The end of a matter is better than its beginning;
Patience of spirit is better than haughtiness of spirit.

In May 2009, Doug and I celebrated thirteen years of marriage. I love my husband more today than ever before. Next to Christ, he is my rock and my best friend! He is supportive and loving. He makes me feel loved and cherished each day. He has walked with me through all of this, steady and holding me up when I felt I could not do it anymore. He understands me and loves me unconditionally. He has allowed his actions to speak louder than his words. He leads our family by example and love.

Lauren broke up with "the boyfriend" in August of 2007. She went through a lot during her first two years away at college, more than I ever wanted her to, however, that is really her story to tell. But I will say I am grateful for her repentant heart. I am grateful God allowed Doug and me to come in at the end of her "prodigal" journey and blind us until she was ready. She has come very far in her life. A huge step she also made was to forgive her father. I am so proud of who she is today. I see the fruit that she bears! She is my angel girl! Exciting news regarding my daughter – in August 2009 she became engaged to a wonderful Godly young man, whom we are proud to call our son-in-law. They will be married in the spring of 2010.

Garic definitely went though his own anxiety worrying about me but I believe his faith is stronger. I know I am a different mother to him than I was to Lauren, not just because I was ten years older when he was born, but because of who I was then and who I am now. I am grateful for our son. He has so much personality. He loves to make us all laugh. He is my sunshine!

All of us are stronger. I am healthy emotionally and spiritually more than I have ever been in my life. It is still a process though. I have to choose each day to give things over to God. I have to be very aware of trigger points. I have to be pro active in protecting myself. I have to have firm boundaries. I have learned to say "No" and know that it is OK. I have also had to learn that I am not responsible for others choices or actions past or present.

My relationship with God is different now. It has been growing and changing over the years. I see God in a completely different light than I did before. I still struggle with self-confidence and self-esteem but God has surrounded me with people who genuinely love and care for me.

Some very exciting news for me is that I found my brother LeRoy after 30 years of wondering what happened to him and searching for him. It was truly Gods perfect timing and purpose. It turns out that I had been misspelling his last name all this time. Through a series of what I consider God-ordained connections and timing, two wonderful friends of mine found information and I was able to connect with my brother. He and I are taking time to get to know one another and I am hopeful that my brother will remain a part of my life.

As I look back through all of my life I can see God's footprints in the sand carrying me along the way. It truly is one day at a time, one situation at a time. My life today is about surrounding myself with good people who will encourage my walk with God, including family, church, and friends, keeping my spiritual armor on, being open and honest, letting my faith grow and not being afraid to stretch and grow. I also need to remember that while growing pains do hurt, in the end it is for the betterment of the body, mind, and heart. Each day is a choice to live the life God has given me to the fullest, and remembering that ultimately, I can only be responsible for my own choices and happiness.

I would like to end with the words to the song…

His Eye is on the Sparrow

Why should I feel discouraged, why should the shadows come,
Why should my heart be lonely, and long for heav'n and home,
When Jesus is my portion? My constant Friend is He:
His eye is on the sparrow, and I know He watches me;
His eye is on the sparrow, and I know He watches me.

I sing because I'm happy, I sing because I'm free,
For His eye is on the sparrow, and I know He watches me.

"Let not your heart be troubled," His tender word I hear,
And resting on His goodness, I lose my doubts and fears;
Though by the path He leadeth, but one step I may see;
His eye is on the sparrow, and I know He watches me;
His eye is on the sparrow, and I know He watches me.

Whenever I am tempted, whenever clouds arise,
When songs give place to sighing, when hope within me dies,
I draw the closer to Him, from care He sets me free;
His eye is on the sparrow, and I know He watches me;
His eye is on the sparrow, and I know He watches me.

My Friends, Thank You

for taking this journey with me.
I would love to hear from you
and how you have been encouraged.
You can contact me at Sheryl@SherylGriffin.com
or P.O. Box 680522 Franklin, TN 37068

If you are interested
in having Sheryl
speak at one of your events please contact her at
Sheryl@SherylGriffin.com

You can keep up with Sheryl on her blog at
www.SherylGriffin.com

LaVergne, TN USA
12 March 2010
175805LV00001B/4/P